Counseling
the
Family of
a
Substance Abuser

**A Work Book & Guide for Counselors
who Work with Families
Dealing With a Member
who is a Substance Abuser**

_____

Compiled and text by
Jim Gordon, Ph.D., MFT #12651
edited by: Christine Keagy, Certified Anger Management Counselor
204 S. Beverly Drive, #116
Beverly Hills, CA 90212
310 271 3784
3rd Edition© 2016
BHCounseling.Com / BeverlyHillsSelfHelp.com / Anger-Online.com
/ GriefandLossBeverlyHills.com

TABLE OF CONTENTS

Foreword

1   UNIT 1   Family therapy

13   UNIT 2   Family Therapy Concepts and Techniques That Substance Abuse Counselors Use

21   UNIT 3   Treatment Models

29   UNIT 4   Therapeutic Models and Levels Recovery

35   UNIT 5   Specific Populations

43   UNIT 6   Focusing on Alcohol and the Drinker - Recognizing and Assessing

53   UNIT 7   Alcohol Problems Framework

61   UNIT 8   Intervention

79   UNIT 9   Intervention II

93   UNIT 10   How Much is Too Much?

101   UNIT 11   Guidelines for Family Violence and Child Abuse Screening

107   Glossary

109   Appendix:

Genograms
The 25-item Alcohol Dependence Scale (ADS)
Severity of Alcohol Dependence Questionnaire (Sadq-c)
Drinker Inventory of Consequences(DrInC)

121   Resources

Dedicated to Ross, Bruce, and Paul.

Dear Readers,

Congratulations on being interested in the Field of Substance Abuse. At some point if you are working in the Field of Mental Health, whether in private practice, or a clinic setting you will, no doubt, have contact with someone who is in a family where there is a Substance Abuser. The abuser might be the IP(Identified Patient) for the family, or your client may be the IP due to their reactions to the abuser. Often the IP for families, will be the most 'sensitive' kid in the family who is now acting out in school and referred to you. That kid is the one who reads the abuser the most honestly, and realizes, dad or mom, brother or sis, doesn't really have the 'flu', or didn't get bitten by a spider, but is DRUNK or stoned. In the meantime, the rest of the family is busy denying and offering excuses. Enabling the abuser.

When counseling kids in such families, you often have to help them 'in spite of' their family, rather than getting help from the family.

This workbook was compiled from many resources dealing with specific parts of the therapy process. I have tried to bring together the basics you will need to not be 'blind-sided' by suddenly finding yourself dealing with the dynamics of the Family of an Abuser. Information is provided for dealing with alcohol and drug abusers. There are many common factors in dealing with alcohol and drug users, however there specific differences such as the very important fact that alcohol is legally available and drugs are not. For instance, drinking at home is legal, but using cocaine in your condo could get you jail time.

I've observed the needs of the folks I have seen over my years practice, as well as what I observed growing up in an alcoholic family - both parents being abusers - one also being a big time prescription drug abuser as well as an alcoholic. I hope to share what I have learned in that journey with you. I have learned from people who have struggled through recovery and those who have not made it, or died in the process. Even though I have been sober all my life (though as my friends know, I'm not sure why,) I have worked at rehab centers from the state hospital based programs to the high end high profile celeb rehabs in Malibu and Hollywood Hills. Again, there are some differences in the types of clients, but much more commonality, whether you are wasted on cheap booze or have your own special 'bump lady'(usually a coke provider) on call, who flies up to your place in Aspen to deliver the goods if you are on a ski trip.

There is no sense in reinventing the wheel, so I have made good use of some wonderful government resources for information also. Please check out sites like www.samhsa.gov, and those listed in the appendix/resource page. Take the time to review the materials, and learn from other's experiences.

Each topic has information explaining and defining it. There are Reflection Questions to probe your thoughts and ideas. Questions for you to push your growth, and a wrap up discussion of the points presented. I hope that by using the information in this workbook you will find creative and helpful solutions when dealing clients problems, as well as those we see in our day to day lives in our own friends, families and colleagues.

Sincerely,

Dr. Jim Gordon
Beverly Hills, CA 2016
BHCounseling.Com / BeverlyHillsSelfHelp.com / Anger-Online.com
GriefandLossBeverlyHills.com

Remembering

UNIT 1

Family Therapy 101

Family Therapy

The family has a central role to play in the treatment of many mental health problems, including substance abuse. Family work has become a strong theme of many treatment approaches including the in-patient re-habs as well as outpatient programs and even heavily impacts 12 steppers. Some schools of thought do focus primarily on the abuser, but more and more programs are broadening the substance abuse treatment focus from the individual to the family, or to at least include the family in some of the treatment.

Though substance abuse counselors usually do not practice family therapy, many of them have the proper training and licensing. Most are encouraged, or in most re-hab centers, they are required, to include family therapy in the re-hab process. They discuss it with their clients and know when a referral is indicated. Substance abuse counselors can also benefit from incorporating family therapy ideas and techniques into their work with individual clients, groups of clients, and family groups.

When it comes to working the clients' family, what is the **definition of a Family**? There is really no single definition of family. However, several broad categories encompass most families: traditional families (two heterosexual parents and minor children all living under the same roof); gay and lesbian couples; single parents; foster parent situation; grandparents raising grandchildren; step-families; extended families, which include grandparents, aunts, uncles, cousins, and other relatives; elected families, which are joined by choice and not by the usual ties of blood, marriage, and law which would include emancipated youth who choose to live among peers, and others living with non-biologically related people with whom they have an emotional tie.

For all practical purposes, the family should be defined according to the individual's closest emotional connections. A counselor or therapist cannot determine which individuals make up the client's family; rather, counselors should ask, "Who is most important to you? Who do you feel closet to and regard as your family?" This allows clients to identify who they think should be included in therapy. Today, with extended families of parents, step-parents, ex's and multiple exes with multiple integrations, many times members of a physically integrated family may feel more closeness and allegiance to someone not living with them such as when they are living at a step parent's house, for instance.

As a therapist, what is the **impact of substance abuse on a family**? First , when a family member abuses substances, the effect on the family may differ according to family structure. Here are some examples:

If Your Client Lives Alone or With Partner - The consequences of substance abuse by an adult who lives alone or with a partner are likely to be economic and psychological. Money may be spent for drug use; the partner who is not using substances often assumes the provider role. Psychological consequences may include denial or protection of the person with the substance use disorder, chronic anger, stress, anxiety, hopelessness, inappropriate sexual behavior, neglected health, shame, stigma, and isolation.

If the Client Lives With Spouse (or Partner) and Minor Children - A parent's substance use can have cognitive, behavioral, psychosocial, and emotional consequences for children, including: impaired learning capacity; a propensity to develop a substance use disorder; adjustment problems, including increased rates of divorce, violence, and the need for control in relationships; other problems such as depression, anxiety, and low self-esteem.

Additionally, the children of women who abuse alcohol during pregnancy are at risk for the effects of fetal alcohol spectrum disorders. Children of those with substance use disorders often feel guilty and responsible for the parent's substance abuse. A simple example, is that parent who screams at their kids, "You drive me to drink." Older children may be forced prematurely to accept adult responsibilities, especially the care of younger siblings when mom or dad are wasted.

If the Client Is Part of a Blended Mixed Family - Many people who abuse substances belong to step-families. Substance abuse can intensify problems and become an impediment to a step-family's integration and stability. When substance abuse is part of the family, unique issues can arise, such as parental authority disputes, sexual or physical abuse, and self-esteem problems for children. Substance abuse by stepparents may undermine their authority, lead to difficulty in forming bonds, and impair a family's ability to address problems and sensitive issues.

The children of integrated blended families often live in and share time in, two different households with different boundaries and the ambiguous roles can be confusing. Without good communication and careful attention to areas of conflict, children may be at increased risk of social, emotional, and behavioral problems.

If an "Older" Client Has Grown Children - Older adults often live with or are supported by their adult children because of financial necessity. Whether grown children and their parents live together or apart, the children must take on a parental, caretaking role. Adjustment to this role reversal can be stressful, painful, and embarrassing.

In some cases, grown children may stop providing financial support because it is the only influence they have over the parent. Adult children often will say to "let them have their little pleasure." In other instances, children may cut ties with the parent because it is too painful watch the parent's deterioration. Cutting ties only increases the parent's isolation and may worsen the substance abuse.

Okay... so what is Family Therapy?

Family therapy is a collection of therapeutic approaches that share a belief in family-level assessment and intervention. A family is a system, and in any system each part is related to all other parts. Consequently, a change in any part of the system will bring about changes in all other parts. Therapy based on this point of view uses the strengths of families to bring about change in a range of diverse problem areas, including substance abuse.

   ** Note always that family therapy can take place only when the safety of all participants can be guaranteed and no legal constraints preclude it. Counselors should have training in handling families with violence and/or neglect. Do NOT try to include members of the family who feel threatened to be included or retaliated against by the abuser or other family member. Guidelines for assessing violence are provided in the APPENDIX.

There are significant differences between substance abuse treatment and family therapy. Although compatible in many ways, the fields of substance abuse treatment and family therapy often use different terms, sometimes understand the same terms differently, have different professional requirements and expectations, and are governed by different assumptions. Some of the basic differences are outlined below.

Family-Involved Therapy vs. Family Therapy

There are also significant differences between family therapy and the "family-involved therapy" which occurs in most substance abuse treatment. Family-involved therapy attempts to educate families about the relationship patterns that typically contribute to the formation and continuation of substance abuse. It differs from family therapy in that the family is not the primary therapeutic grouping, nor is there intervention in the system of family relationships. Most substance abuse treatment centers offer such a family educational approach. It is not based on, nor focused on, family problems such as the children's behavior or school problems, or intimacy issues between the spouse and partners, but based on the dynamics of having a substance abuser in a family and how it impacts and affects the family dynamic.

In substance abuse treatment, the term **denial** is generally used to describe a common and complex reaction of people with substance use disorders who, when confronted with the existence of those disorders, deny having the problem. Family therapists' understanding of the term denial will vary more according to the particular therapist's theoretical orientation. Some may see it as a strategy for maintaining stability and therefore not a problem at all.

Many substance abuse treatment counselors base their understanding of a family's relation to substance abuse on a **disease model.** Within this model, practitioners have come to appreciate substance abuse as a "family disease" - a disease that affects all members of a family as a result of the substance abuse of one or more members and that creates negative changes in their own moods, behaviors, relationships with the family, and sometimes even physical or emotional health.

The Couple and Family: Alcohol Problems

When someone experiences alcohol problems, the negative effects of drinking exert a toll, not only on the drinker, but also on their partner and other family members. Recent data suggest that approximately one child in every four (28.6%) in the United States is exposed to alcohol abuse or dependence in the family. One of the clearest demonstrations of how alcohol use negatively impacts the family is the widely documented association between alcohol use and interpersonal violence.

Family problems that are likely to co-occur with alcohol problems include:
        Violence
        Marital conflict
        Infidelity
        Jealousy
        Economic insecurity
        Divorce
        Fetal alcohol effects

6

Drinking problems may negatively alter marital and family functioning, but there also is evidence that they can increase as a consequence of marital and family problems. Thus, drinking and family functioning are strongly and reciprocally linked. Not surprisingly, alcohol problems are common in couples that present for marital therapy, and marital problems are common in drinkers who present for alcohol treatment.

Family therapists, on the other hand, for the most part have adopted a **family systems model**. It conceptualizes substance abuse as a symptom of dysfunction in the family - a relatively stable symptom because in some way it serves a purpose in the family system. It is this focus on the family system, more than the inclusion of more people, which defines family therapy.

Family **intervention** in substance abuse treatment typically refers to a confrontation that a group of family and friends have with a person abusing substances. Their goal is to convey the impact of the substance abuse and to urge entry into treatment. The treatment itself is likely to be shorter and more time-limited than that of a family therapist, who will focus more on intrafamily relationships in an effort to improve family functioning.

The term **spirituality** plays a large part in the substance abuse programs. In part because of the role of spirituality in 12-Step groups, substance abuse treatment providers generally consider a spiritual emphasis more important than do family therapists. Family therapy developed from the mental health medical field, and as such the emphasis on the scientific underpinnings to medical practice has reduced the role of spirituality, especially in theory and largely in clinical practice.

Process and Content: Compared to substance abuse counselors, family therapists tend to focus more on the <u>process</u> of family interactions and the dynamics among family members than on the <u>content</u> of each session. For example, a family therapist might comment more on how family members ignore or pay attention to one another in conversation, rather than what specifically was being discussed.

Focus: The focus for substance abuse counselors is the **substance abuse and the abuser**. For family therapists, it is **the family system and all its members** and their impact on the abuser and vice-versa.

IP: Who is the client, the **IP (Identified Patient)**? Most often the substance abuse counselor regards the individual with the substance use disorder as the primary person requiring treatment (though the family may be involved in treatment to some degree). The family therapy community assumes that if long-term change is to occur, the entire family must be treated as a unit, so the family as a whole constitutes the client. Often in many cases, the IP can be the acting out kid who came to the attention of their school for bad behavior.

Self-disclosure: How is **self-disclosure by the counselor** handled? Many people who have been in recovery for some time and who have experience in self-help groups have become paraprofessional or professional treatment providers. As a result, it is common for substance abuse treatment counselors to disclose information about their own experiences with recovery. Clients in substance abuse treatment often have some previous contact with self-help groups, and usually feel comfortable with counselors' self-disclosure.

The practice of sharing personal history receives much less emphasis in family therapy. In family therapy, self-disclosure is downplayed because it takes the focus of therapy off of the family. In training for family therapy, as well as clinical psychology and clinical social work, most schools of thought strongly recommend no self disclosure. Their thought being that by self-disclosing, the client now has information about the therapist, and can, and often does, re-direct the attention from the client back onto the therapist! It gives the client a tool, by being able to talk about the therapist's life and interests and take the pressure of the client themselves. In substance abuse counseling, the self-disclosure is used more to align the client and the therapist/counselor, so the client feels the therapist has also been down the same road, so they will understand what the client is going through.

Study Questions

1. For practical purposes, a family can be defined as:
   a. the individual's closest emotional connections.
   b. what the counselor or therapist can determine make up the client's family
   c. two heterosexual parents and siblings from those same parents
   d. what is defined by law as family
   e. what is defined by the church as family.

2. The primary consequences of substance abuse by an adult who lives with a partner are likely to be:

a. economic

b. psychological

c. social

d. none of the above

e. a and b

3. A parent's substance use can have cognitive, behavioral, psychosocial, and emotional consequences for children, resulting in:

    a. Impaired learning capacity

    b. A propensity to develop a substance use disorder

    c. Adjustment problems, including increased rates of divorce, violence, and the need for control in relationships

    d. Other problems such as depression, anxiety, and low self-esteem

    e. All of the above

4. When substance abuse is part of a family, unique issues can arise, such as parental authority disputes, sexual or physical abuse, and self esteem problems for children. Substance abuse by stepparents may:

    a. undermine their authority

    b. lead to difficulty in forming bonds

    c. impair a family's ability to address problems and sensitive issues.

    d. All of the above

    e. none of the above

5. In dealing with abusers, the primary issue in establishing if Family Therapy can take place is:

    a. that it be done in a comfortable, non-threatening environment.

    b. that it be done with a flexible schedule to accommodate all family members.

    c. whether the family meets the legal definition of family

    d. if the other members of the family are either sober or achieving sobriety

    e. that the safety of all participants can be guaranteed and no legal constraints preclude it.

6. A family is a system, and in any system each part is related to all other parts. Consequently, a change in any part of the system will bring about changes in all other parts. Therapy based on this point of view uses:

    a. childhood analysis to get to the root of the members of the systems problems first.

    b. genograms exclusively and extensively for empirical analysis of the family system.

    c. astrology to interpret the next mood swing.

d. the strengths of families to bring about change in a range of diverse problem areas, including substance abuse.

e. therapy to explore past family history to establish if abuse is genetic in this family, thus negating the use of talk therapy since it's a chronic issue.

7. What is the prime factor that differentiates between Family-involved Therapy and Family Therapy?

a. It differs from family therapy in that the family is not the primary therapeutic grouping, nor is there intervention in the system of family relationships.

b. It differs from family therapy in that the family becomes the primary therapeutic grouping by getting everyone involved and responsible for the abusers recovery.

c. It does NOT involve time consuming and often unproductive interventions.

d. It is based on inpatient rehab for the abuser with the family participating in family sessions.

e. Who cares?

8. A great many Substance Abuse Treatment Counselors, as well as programs like NA, CA, and AA, base their understanding of a family's relation to substance abuse on what model?

a. Janice Dickenson's models

b. Jungian model

c. chronic model

d. disease model

e. systems theory model.

9. The majority of Family Therapists base their understanding of a family's relation to substance abuse on what model?

a. Janice Dickenson's models

b. Jungian model

c. chronic model

d. disease model

e. systems theory model.

10. In substance abuse treatment there typically is a confrontation that a group of family and friends have with a person abusing substances. Their goal is to convey the impact of the substance abuse and to urge entry into treatment. What is this 'confrontation' called?

a. family conference

b. family therapy
c. family home evening
d. family intervention
e. family system

11. Which of the following is the most correct statement?
    a. The focus for substance abuse counselors is prevention and education. For family therapists, it is the family system.
    b. The focus for substance abuse counselors is the substance abuse. For family therapists, it is the analysis of the abusers pathology.
    c. The focus for substance abuse counselors is the substance abuse. For family therapists, it is the family system. Period.
    d. The focus for substance abuse counselors is the recovery. For family therapists, it is the working with the family to enable the recovery.

12. Regarding, Self-Disclosure by the Counselor, many people who have been in recovery for some time and who have experience in self-help groups have become paraprofessional or professional treatment providers. As a result, it is common for substance abuse treatment counselors to disclose information about their own experiences with recovery. Clients in substance abuse treatment often have some previous contact with self-help groups, and usually feel comfortable with counselors' self-disclosure.
    True   False

Notes:

UNIT 2

Family Therapy Concepts
and
Techniques That
Substance Abuse Counselors Use

Family Therapy Concepts and Techniques That Substance Abuse Counselors Use

The field of **Family Therapy** has developed a number of theoretical concepts and techniques that can help substance abuse treatment providers to better understand clients' relationships with their families.

Complementarity. Complementarity refers to an interactional pattern in which members of an intimate relationship establish roles and take on behavioral patterns that fulfill the unconscious needs and demands of the other. An implication when treating substance abuse is that the results of one family member's recovery need to be explored in relation to the rest of the family's behavior.

Boundaries. Boundaries delineate one family member from another, generations within families, or the family from other systems. Boundaries also regulate the flow of information in the family and between systems outside the family.

Dysfunctional patterns can arise in boundaries ranging from extremes of enmeshment (smotheringly close) to disengagement (unreachably aloof). When boundaries are too strong, family members can become disengaged and the family will lack the cohesion needed to hold itself together. When boundaries are too weak, family members can become psychologically and emotionally enmeshed and lose their ability to act as individuals.

Appropriate boundaries vary from culture to culture, and the clinician needs to consider whether a pattern of disengagement or enmeshment is a function of culture or pathology.

Subsystems. Within a family system, subsystems are separated by clearly defined boundaries that fulfill particular functions. These subsystems have their own roles and rules within the family system. For example, in a healthy family, a parental subsystem (which can be made up of one or more individual members) maintains a degree of privacy, assumes responsibility for providing for the family, and has power to make decisions for the family. These subsystem rules and expectations can have a strong impact on client behavior and can be used to motivate or influence a client in a positive direction.

Enduring Family Ties. Another important principle of family therapy is that families are connected through more than physical proximity and frequent interactions.

Strong emotional ties connect family members, even when they are separated. It is possible to involve a client in a form of family therapy even if family members are not physically present.

Change and Balance. Family rules and scripts are not unchangeable, but families exhibit different degrees of adaptability when faced with the need to change patterns of behavior. A tendency in all families is <u>homeostasis</u>—a state of equilibrium that balances strong, competing forces in families as they tend to resist change—that must be overcome if change is to occur. In order to function well, families need to be able to preserve order and stability without becoming too rigid to adapt.

Adjusting to Abstinence. The family of a client who has a substance use disorder can be expected to act differently (and not always positively) when the individual with a substance use disorder enters recovery. A family may react negatively to an individual member's cessation of substance use (e.g., children may behave more aggressively or lie and steal to regain homeostasis), or there may be a period of relative harmony that is disrupted when other problems that have been suppressed begin to surface.

If these other problems are not dealt with, the family's reactions may trigger relapse. Family therapy techniques can resolve problems formerly masked by substance abuse to ensure that the family helps, rather than hinders, a client's long-term recovery.

Triangulation. Triangulation occurs when two family members need to discuss a sensitive issue. Instead of facing the issue, they divert their energy to a third member who acts as a go-between, scapegoat, object of concern, or ally. By involving this other person, they reduce their emotional tension, but prevent their conflict from being resolved and miss opportunities to increase the intimacy in their relationship.

In families organized around substance abuse, a common pattern is for one parent to be closely allied with a child while the other parent remains distant. Triangulation is especially common in families that are highly enmeshed, but it does occur to some extent in all families.

The third party in a triangle need not be a family member. Counselors should be aware of the possibility of becoming involved in a triangle with clients by competing with the client's family over the client. This process is especially common in programs that treat only the client without involving the family. Even the substance in the abuse can also be considered an entity with which the client triangulates to avoid deeper levels of intimacy, i.e, blames the "demon run", or that they "live their life for their next hit of coke."

Integrated Treatment: Benefits, Limitations, and Levels of Involvement with Families

Benefits to Clients

Examining substance use disorders through the dynamics of the whole family has a number of advantages:

<u>Treatment outcomes</u>. Family involvement in substance abuse treatment is positively associated with increased rates of entry into treatment, decreased dropout rates during treatment, and better long-term outcomes.

<u>Client recovery</u>. When family members understand how they have participated in the client's substance abuse and are willing to actively support the client's recovery, the likelihood of successful, long-term recovery improves.

<u>Family recovery</u>. When families are involved in treatment, the focus can be on the larger family issues, not just the substance abuse.

<u>Intergenerational impact</u>. Integrated models can help reduce the impact and recurrence of substance use disorders in different generations.

Benefits to Therapists/Counselors

In addition to the benefits for clients and their families, integrated models are advantageous to treatment providers. The practical advantages include:

<u>Reduced resistance</u>. Integrated models permit counselors to attend to the specific circumstances of each family in treatment, thus reducing resistance.

<u>Flexibility in treatment planning</u>. Integrated models enable counselors to tailor treatment plans to reflect individual and family factors.

<u>Flexibility in treatment approach</u>. Integrated models enable counselors to adjust treatment approaches according to their own personal styles and strengths. In this way, different treatment models can be used even within the same agency to meet both client and counselor needs.

<u>Increased skill set</u>. Drawing from different traditional therapy models challenges counselors to be creative in their treatment approaches. With integrated models, for instance, substance abuse treatment counselors can work with family members and see how each of their problems reverberates throughout the family system.

Some of the Limitations of Integrating Treatment

Despite the obvious value and demonstrated efficacy, integrated models for substance abuse treatment have some limitations which include the following.

Involvement with Families There can be a <u>lack of structure</u>. If the various modalities in integrated models are not consistent and compatible, the combination can end up as little more than a series of disconnected interventions.

Often new counselors, peer counselors and even seasoned counselor and therapists need <u>additional training</u>. Integrated models require greater knowledge of more treatment modalities, so additional training is necessary and knowledge of resources.

The major <u>mindset shift</u> necessary to using integrated models is from an individual model concentrating on pathology to a systemic (relational or behavioral) model focused on changing patterns of family interaction. Counselors who come from a clinical psychology model often have the most problem since they are trained to work with the individual **inspite** of their surroundings and to help the person become the most functional. Working with the conglomerate family unit can be very different for 'individual' counselors and therapists.

The Levels of Involvement with Families

Substance abuse treatment professionals intervene with families at different levels during treatment. These levels vary according to how individualized the interventions are to each family, the extent to which the substance abuse treatment provider is trained and supervised in family therapy techniques, and the extent to which family therapy is integrated into the process of substance abuse treatment.

At each level, family intervention has a different function and requires its own set of competencies. The family's acceptance of problems and its 'readiness to change' determine the appropriate level of counselor involvement with that family.

Level 1 - Counselor has little or no involvement with family.
- The counselor contacts families for practical and legal reasons and provides no services to them
- The counselor views the individual in treatment as the only client and may even feel that during treatment, the client must be protected from family contact

Level 2 - Counselor provides psycho education and advice. Typical skills:
- Advising families about how to handle the rehabilitative needs of the client

- For large or demanding families, knowing how to channel communication through one or two key members
- Identifying gross family dysfunction that interferes with substance abuse treatment
- Referring the family for specialized family therapy treatment

Level 3 - Counselor addresses family members' feelings and provides support. Typical skills:

- Asking questions that elicit family members' expressions of concern and feelings related to the client's condition and its effect on the family
- Empathically listening to family members' concerns and feelings and, where appropriate, normalizing them
- Forming a preliminary assessment of the family's level of functioning as it relates to the client's problem
- Encouraging family members in their efforts to cope with their situation as a family
- Tailoring substance abuse education to the unique needs, concerns, and feelings of the family
- Identifying family dysfunction and fitting referral recommendations to the unique situation of the family

Level 4 - Counselor provides systematic assessment and planned intervention. Typical skills:

- Engaging family members, including reluctant ones, in a planned family conference or a series of conferences
- Structuring a conference with even a poorly communicating family in such a way that all members have a chance to express themselves
- Systematically assessing the family's level of functioning
- Supporting individual members while avoiding coalitions
- Re-framing the family's definition of its problem in a way that makes problem solving more achievable
- Helping family members view their difficulties as requiring new forms of collaborative efforts
- Helping family members generate alternative, mutually acceptable ways to cope with difficulties
- Helping the family balance its coping efforts by calibrating various roles so that members can support each other without sacrificing autonomy
- Identifying family dysfunction beyond the scope of primary care treatment; orchestrating a referral by informing the family and the specialist about what to expect from each other

Level 5 - Family therapy. Typical skills:
- Interviewing families or family members who are difficult to engage
- Efficiently generating and testing hypotheses about the family's difficulties and interaction patterns
- Escalating conflict in the family in order to break a family impasse
- Temporarily siding with one family member against another
- Constructively dealing with a family's strong resistance to change
- Negotiating collaborative relationships with professionals from other systems that are working with the family, even when these groups are at odds with one another

Notes:

UNIT 3

Treatment Models

Treatment Models

Here are the basic Treatment Models used in the field of counseling and how they work with, or fit into, the Family of a Substance Abuser type of counseling situation. If you are a student with a goal of social work, or therapy in general, you have been exposed in other classes to many of these integrated treatment models. These are the most frequently used integrated treatment models in dealing with substance abuse but remember there are other options.

Structural/Strategic Family Therapy

In this model, family structure (defined as repeated patterns of interaction) is the focus of interventions. It is based on two assumptions:
- Family structure largely determines individual behavior
- The power of the system is greater than the ability of the individual to resist

This system can be used to identify the function that substance abuse serves in maintaining family stability. Guide appropriate changes in family structure (e.g., because the patterns in dysfunctional families are typically rigid, the counselor must take a directive role and coach family members to develop, then practice, different patterns of interaction).

One of the basic techniques of structural family therapy is to mark boundaries so that each member of the family can be responsible for him- or herself while respecting the individuality of others. One of the ways to make respectful individuation possible is to make the family aware when a family member speaks about, rather than to, another person who is present, speaks for others, instead of letting them speak for themselves, sends nonverbal cues to influence or stop another person from speaking

Multidimensional Family Therapy

Multidimensional family therapy (MDFT) was developed as an outpatient therapy to treat adolescent substance abuse and associated behavioral problems of clinically referred teenagers. The model integrates several different techniques with emphasis on the relationships among cognition, affect (emotionality), behavior, and environmental input.

With adolescents who abuse substances, the goals include:
- Positive peer relations
- Healthy identity formation
- Bonding to school and other pro-social institutions
- Autonomy within the parent–adolescent relationship

For parents, the goals are:
- Increasing parental commitment and preventing parental abdication
- Improving relationship and communication between parent and adolescent
- Increasing knowledge of parenting practices (e.g., limit-setting, monitoring, and appropriate autonomy granting)

Behavioral Family Therapy and/or Cognitive - Behavioral Family Therapy CBT

Behavioral Family Therapy (BFT) combines individual interventions within a family problem solving framework. The approach assumes that:
- families of people abusing substances may have problem solving skill deficits
- The reactions of other family members influence behavior
- Distorted beliefs lead to dysfunction and distorted behaviors
- Therapy helps family members develop behaviors that support non-using and non-drinking
- Over time, these new behaviors become more and more rewarding, promoting abstinence

Cognitive Behavioral Family Therapy views substance abuse as a conditioned behavioral response, one which family cues and contingencies reinforce. To facilitate behavioral change within a family to support abstinence, the CBT counselor can utilize the following CBT techniques:
1. Contingency contracting. These agreements stipulate what each member will do in exchange for rewarding behavior from other family members. For example, a teenager may agree to call home regularly while attending a concert in exchange for permission to attend it.
2. Skills training. The counselor may start with general education about communication or conflict resolution skills, then move to skills practice during therapy, and end with the family's agreement to use the skills at home.
3. Cognitive restructuring. The counselor helps family members voice unrealistic

or self-limiting beliefs that contribute to substance abuse or other family problems. Family members are encouraged to see how such beliefs threaten ongoing recovery and family tranquility. Finally, the family is helped to replace these self-defeating beliefs with those that facilitate recovery and individual and family strengths.

Family and Larger System - Case Management Therapy

This model is primarily for families who are or should be involved intensely with larger systems (the workplace, schools, health care, courts, foster care, etc.) The goal is to empower the family in working with the larger system by designating the family as the major expert on its own needs. Counselors help the family navigate various systems, serving to some extent as a community liaison.

Counselors utilizing this model will need to determine, what larger systems affect the family? What agencies and agency subsystems regularly interact with family members? How is the family moved from one larger system to another? Is there a history of significant involvement with larger systems, and if so, regarding what issues?

For example, families with substance abuse problems interact more regularly with the judicial system, because of arrests (e.g., for driving under the influence, loss of parental rights, and domestic violence).

Network Therapy

Network therapy utilizes the potential of therapeutic support from people outside the immediate family, including friends, extended family, and 12Step groups such as Alcoholics Anonymous (AA). The counselor works to mobilize the client's network, to keep the people in the network informed and involved, and to encourage the client to accept help from the network.

As you all probably are aware from friends and family, and in some cases, your own situations, AA and its associated programs (AA, NA, CA, Al-Anon, Overeaters Anon, etc.) are the usual 'first referral' and 'front guard' for most abuse situations. Even if more involved therapies are used, the 12 step programs should not be forgotten and can be used in conjunction with, other therapies.

Bowen Family Systems Therapy

Bowen family systems therapy often works through one person, on the premise that a change on the part of just one family member will affect the family system. The model attempts to reduce anxiety throughout the family by encouraging people to become more differentiated, more autonomous, and less enmeshed in the family emotional system.

In Bowen's view, specific and problematic anxiety and relationship patterns are handed down from generation to generation. Some inter-generational patterns that may require therapeutic focus are:

1. **Creating distance**. Alcohol and drugs are used to manage anxiety by creating distance in the family.
2. **Triangulation**. Triangulation is an emotional pattern that can involve either three people or two people and an issue (such as the substance abuse). In the latter situation, the substance is used to displace anxiety that exists between the two people.
3. **Coping**. Substance abuse is used to mute emotional responses to family members and to create a false sense of family equilibrium.

Solution-Focused Brief Therapy

Rather than focusing on an extensive description of the problem, solution-focused brief therapy (SFBT) encourages client and therapist to focus instead on what life will be like when the problem is solved. The emphasis is on the development of a solution in the future, rather than on understanding the development of the problem in the past or its maintenance in the present. Exceptions to the problem—that is, times when the problem does not happen and a piece of the future solution is present—are elicited and built on.

Perhaps the most representative of the SFBT techniques is the "miracle question", which elicits clients' vision of life without the problems that brought them to therapy. Bowen's "miracle question" traditionally takes this form:

"Suppose that while you are sleeping tonight, and the entire house is quiet, a miracle happens: The problem that you came here for has been solved. Because you are sleeping, however, you don't know that the miracle has happened. When you wake up tomorrow morning, what will be different that will tell you a miracle has occurred, and that your problem has been solved?"

The miracle question serves several purposes. It helps the client imagine what life would be like if his or her problems were solved, gives hope of change, and previews the benefits of that change. Its most important feature, however, is its transfer of power to clients. It permits them to create their own vision of the change they want. It does not require them to accept a vision composed or suggested by an expert.

Notes:

UNIT 4

Therapeutic Models
and
Levels Recovery

Therapeutic Models and Levels of Recovery

Families have to learn to cope with all THREE levels of Sobriety that the abuser(IP) has achieved, or is going through! There are different issues at each point. AND the therapists/counselors have to be tuned in and aware of these levels and the idiosyncrasies that go with each for total success.

Here are the three different accepted levels in the progression of treatment:

Attainment of Sobriety: The family system is unbalanced but healthy change is possible.

Adjustment to Sobriety: The family works on developing and stabilizing a new system.

Long-term Maintenance of Sobriety: The family must re-balance and stabilize a new and healthier lifestyle.

How do you determine what level of recovery the family has reached so you can help the family and focus your counseling?

1. Interview the family in relation to the larger system.
2. Interview the family and people in other larger systems that assist the family.
3. Interview larger system representatives (e.g., school counselors, colleagues at work) without the family present (provided that issues of confidentiality have been addressed).

The following are a brief description of what and how each of the listed **Theories** would affect the person at the different Levels, and suggests the benefits of their use at each Level of Sobriety. Remember there are no concrete rules for sobriety, you have to be flexible and prepared for anything.

Level One: Attainment of Sobriety

Bowen Family Systems Therapy emphasizes and encourages:

• Reduced levels of anxiety.
• Creating a Genogram (see appendix) showing multi-generational substance abuse;

31

explore family disruption from system events, such as immigration or holocaust.
• Orienting the nuclear family toward facts versus reactions by using factual questioning.
• Altering triangulation by coaching families to take different interactional positions.
• Asking individual family members more questions, so the whole family learns more about itself.

Multidimensional Family Therapy emphasizes and encourages:

• Motivating family to engage client in detoxification.
• Contracting with the family for abstinence.
• Contracting with the family regarding its own treatment.
• Defining problems and contract with family members to curtail the problems.
• Employing Al-Anon, spousal support groups, and multifamily support groups.

Behavioral Family Therapy emphasizes and encourages:

• Conducting community reinforcement training interviews (e.g., with area clergy to help them develop ways to impact the community).

Network and Family/Larger System emphasizes and encourages:

• Using the network (including courts, parole officers, employer, team staff, licensing boards, child protective services, social services, lawyers, schools, etc.) to motivate treatment.
• Interviewing the family in relation to the larger system.
• Interviewing the family and people in other larger systems that assist the family.
• Interviewing larger system representatives (e.g., school counselors) without the family present (provided that issues of confidentiality have been addressed).

Level Two: Adjustment to Sobriety

Structural/Strategic Systems emphasizes and encourages:

• Restructuring family roles (the main work of this model).

• Realign subsystem and generational boundaries.
• Reestablish boundaries between the family and the outside world.

Multidimensional Family Therapy emphasizes and encourages:

• Efforts to stabilize the family.
• Reorganizing the family.
• Teaching relapse prevention.
• Identifying communication dysfunction.
• Teaching communication and conflict resolution skills.
• Assessing developmental stages of each person in the family.
• Considering family system interactions based on personality disorders.
• Considering whether to refer to an appropriate professional to assess if medication is needed for depression, anxiety, or posttraumatic stress disorder.
• Considering whether to address loss and mourning, along with sexual or physical abuse.

Cognitive–Behavioral Family Therapy emphasizes and encourages:

• Conducting community reinforcement training interviews.
• Establishing a problem definition.
• Employing structure and strategy.
• Using communication skills and negotiation skills training.
• Employing conflict resolution techniques.
• Using contingency contracting.

Network Interventions emphasizes and encourages:

• Using organizations such as AA, Al-Anon, Alateen, and Families Anonymous as part of the network.
• Delineating and redistribute tasks among all service providers working with the family.
• Using rituals when clients are receiving simultaneous and conflicting messages.

Solution-Focused Family Therapy emphasizes and encourages:

• Employing the miracle question.
• Asking scaling and relational questions.
• Identifying exceptions to problem behavior.

• Identifying problem and solution sequences.

Level Three: Long-Term Maintenance of Sobriety

Family/Larger Systems/Case Management emphasizes and encourages:

• Renegotiating relationships with larger systems (e.g., agree with Child Protective Services that once the family has completed treatment, the child/children can be returned to the home).

Network Therapy emphasizes and encourages:

• Utilizing Al-Anon, spousal support groups, and multifamily support groups.

Notes:

UNIT 5

Understanding Specifics
of the Population

Understanding Specifics of the Population

An understanding and awareness of this section is very important. While there are many commonalities to working with substance abusers of all segments of the world, there are some specifics that need to be noted in working with different segments of the population. Times change, and as you continue to work in counseling, you need to keep abreast of changes that happen in society and its segments. Women's roles have changed drastically over the past 30+ years. Gay, Bisexual and Lesbian folks have become more mainstream. Racial and ethnic minorities in many cases and areas of the country have become the majorities. You, as a therapist have to be aware of these changes and how they may require adjustment.

For instance, while there are many AA meetings for Gay Men only, more and more you will find Gay, Lesbians and Bisexuals in mixed AA meetings. And as a counselor, you will have more and more chance of finding more openness in family counseling about sexuality. Recently, I dealt with a Korean family who had to confront the fact that their son is gay, an alcoholic and diagnosed with AIDS all in our first family session! I had to be sensitive to their cultural issues 150%. I have worked with the culture many times, and had sensitivity toward their issues of honor and respect.

You will need to be ready to ask for help, do some quick research On-line! Resources like Google are a wonder today. You can type in "Russian attitude toward cocaine abuse" and have an evening of reading. Take the time to do the research, it will help you AND help the client.

What is presented here is just a teaser, and are not the final, nor definitive rules for dealing with populations, but just a teaser. You have to do the rest of the research.

Women

Family therapy for women with substance use disorders is appropriate except in cases in which there is ongoing partner abuse. Safety should always be the primary consideration. This could mean that the abusive partner progresses through treatment directed at impulse control or a batterers' program before any family or couples therapy is initiated.

Racial and Ethnic Minorities

A great deal of research exists on both family therapy and culture and ethnicity. Utilize it. Much of the recent research has concentrated on how culture and ethnicity influence core family and clinical processes. Many cultures still find "therapy" only for crazies! And there is a big resistance to allowing help. Be tuned into those things.

Generalizations about barriers to treatment for racially and ethnically diverse men and women should be made with caution. Nevertheless, some barriers to treatment, particularly among African Americans and Hispanics/Latinos, have been investigated.

Some issues include but are not limited to:
- Problem recognition or perceptions of problem severity
- Doubt about the efficacy of treatment
- Inaccurate perceptions about the cost or availability of treatment (especially for people who lack insurance)
- A cultural need to maintain dignity
- Negative beliefs about treatment (e.g., harsh rules in residential programs)
- Structural problems (e.g., too little treatment for people with no or inadequate insurance, inadequate detoxification facilities, bureaucratic red tape)

Gay, Lesbian, and Bisexual Clients

Unfortunately, statistics show a higher incidence of drug and alcohol use in the Gay, Lesbian and Bisexual population. In larger cities where there are GLBT organizations there are often media blitzes as there is in West Hollywood about Substance Abuse. West Hollywood has special task forces targeting Crystal Meth use for instance.

Research is insufficient to suggest the efficacy of any one type of family therapy over another for use with gay and lesbian clients, but more important than the school of therapy is the therapist's knowledge, understanding, and acceptance of differing sexual orientations. Treatment providers often are not trained in the specific needs of these populations, even though gay, lesbian, and bisexual individuals in treatment for substance abuse often take part in family therapy.

People with Physical or Cognitive Disabilities

The life challenges facing family members with disabilities increases their risk of substance use, makes treatment more complex, and heightens the possibility of relapse.

Because family members may feel responsible for the individual's condition and present mostly with negativity, providers must address guilt and anger. Researchers suggest that a therapist assist both the family and the member with a disability to focus on the choices at their disposal. Such questions as "What are you doing that perpetuates the situation?" and "Are you aware of other choices that would have a different result?" can empower clients to understand that they retain the powerful option of making choices.

A strengths-based approach to treatment is especially important for people with disabilities, because such clients may have so frequently been viewed in terms of what they cannot or should not attempt that they may have learned to define themselves in terms of their limitations and inabilities. Well-intentioned family members and friends may encourage dependence and may even feel threatened when the member with a disability attempts to achieve a measure of independence.

Children and Adolescents

Providers will need to make accommodations for children in therapy (e.g., children should not be left too long in the waiting room and should not be expected to sit still for an hour while adult conversation takes place around them). Parents can be taught techniques to decrease reactivity and ways to provide real and acceptable choices for their children.

Children can be encouraged to handle developmentally appropriate tasks and to understand that outcomes are tied to behavior. Moving therapy from the clinic to settings with which an adolescent is familiar and comfortable can be helpful. Conducting sessions at an adolescent's home may promote a more open and sharing tone than sessions in an office. Scheduling of sessions must be sensitive not only to school obligations, but to extracurricular and social activities as well.

Gender also may have implications in family groupings, particularly in families where abuse has occurred. There may be cases where father/son or mother/daughter sessions will be helpful.

Ultimately, treatment for adolescents and children is challenging and may require referral. Utilize this last item please, refer the kids to someone who understands their issues if you are not tuned in to adolescents and children. The kids are resilient, yet fragile, an oxymoron, but reality. Be careful.

Older Adults

Many students are going into Gerontology as a career. During your education, you will become more and more sensitive to the needs of this burgeoning population. Today we are making more of an effort to examine the older adults and the efficacy of family therapy to treat older adults. Some indications suggest it is an effective method to draw even the older person who lives alone back into a family context and reduce feelings of isolation. At the same time, the therapist must respect the elder's autonomy and privacy, and obtain specific permission from the client to contact family members and communicate with them about substance abuse problems. The therapist also should be aware that adult children may have their own substance use problems and screen them carefully.

Therapists must be sensitive to the possibility of elder abuse, which is pervasive, though often overlooked. In some States, it is mandatory for all helping professionals to report elder abuse.

Rural and Outlying Populations

The geographic dispersion of families in rural areas may require them to travel great distances in order to access treatment. A provider has several options for addressing distance barriers: Contract with the family for a limited number of sessions and be very focused in the work; Alternate sessions at the office with sessions at the client's home or choose a location in between (e.g., a local church or community center); Schedule extended sessions that allow bigger chunks of therapeutic work to occur every 2 or 3 weeks instead of weekly.

Homeless Clients

For those of you who will work in Metropolitan areas, dealing with the Homeless Population will become routine. For instance, recently while I was on patrol with the Sheriff Volunteers, we saw an older gentleman get off the city bus near one of the upscale nightclubs in the city. Shortly we got called over to deal with him. He was very inebriated, was soliciting funds from the patron on the outdoor patio. When we approached him, he laid down on the ground and said out loud, "I can't breathe, I need the paramedics." With that, we were obligated to radio dispatch and have paramedics and an ambulance respond. We talked with him while the first responders were prepping him for transportation to our hospital. He explained he was feeling sick, tired and very hungry, so he took the bus from his downtown ghetto to our city where he knew we would send him to our local hospital. He did not want to go to the downtown county hospital. This gentleman knew the ropes and used them. He was a person with no family, and a limited future.

Many homeless people do not have a family group to bring into therapy, even by the most inclusive interpretations. Still, family dynamics remain integral to the functioning of even the most isolated individuals, and one-person family therapy may be an effective approach in substance abuse treatment if family members are not reachable or amenable to being in treatment.

Veterans

This is another population that is getting looked at more and more with the Vietnam Vets, Iraq War returnees, and Gulf War Vets having their problems. Limited specific family therapy research about veteran populations exists however, most of the research is based on their military history and is done through Veteran Hospitals. As a therapist, you can help the veteran locate services, including benefits to which they are entitled. Therapists also need to know where local veteran centers are. If treatment is difficult to access, it may be hard to get families involved. Here is a case where the therapist can learn and make use of the VA resources yourself. Talk with their case managers, social workers. Most VA centers and organizations are more than willing to help you understand their clients.

Veterans' wives, particularly, may need support, and support groups can be helpful. Children may face a number of issues related to a parent's veteran status.

The issue of abandoned children may also be difficult for veterans. A number of veterans fathered children while in the service, and these lost families often need to be addressed in family therapy.

41

UNIT 6

Focusing on Alcohol and the Drinker - Recognizing & Assessing

Focusing on Alcohol and the Drinker
- Recognizing & Assessing -

While drugs and alcohol can be lumped together under "Substance Abuse", Alcohol and its "drinkers" have some of their own factors. At this point in the book, we will focus more on the drinker, and the drinker's family.

Alcohol Problem Assessment

Screening for alcohol problems should be considered only a first step. Screening alone does not provide enough information to make either a diagnosis or an informed treatment decision. If an individual or family screens positive, i.e. there are indications of risk, further assessment is required to confirm the problem and to determine its nature, extent, and severity. Since screening instruments are designed to err on the side of inclusion, (i.e., to maximize sensitivity rather than specificity), the initial goal of a more intensive problem assessment is to confirm or rule out the presence of an alcohol problem.

The next step in the process is to choose an intervention strategy that matches the nature of the identified problem. By broadening the target population for alcohol-related interventions to include people with risky drinking patterns and mild to moderate alcohol problems, you will address a wider range of concerns that families may have about drinking. The goal of treatment also is necessarily broadened. From an alcohol problems framework, the overall goal of treatment is "To reduce or eliminate the use of alcohol as a contributing factor to physical, psychological, and social dysfunction and to arrest, retard, or reverse the progress of associated problems."

Identifying Alcohol Problems

To achieve this treatment goal and effectively reach the large numbers of individuals and families manifesting mild or moderate alcohol problems, brief interventions are recommended. Brief interventions are time-limited strategies that focus on reducing alcohol use and thereby minimize the risks associated with drinking. Several studies have substantiated the effectiveness of brief interventions for non-dependent problem drinkers. They also are used for more serious alcohol problems, either as the sole intervention, or as the initial step toward longer or more intensive treatment. Although most brief interventions use a cognitive-behavioral approach, you can integrate these interventions into your overall treatment model, regardless of your theoretical orientation.

Once you have identified an alcohol problem and have determined that a brief intervention approach would be appropriate, you are faced with a series of clinical decisions. The next sections of this Guide will walk you through the steps required to achieve a successful response from an individual, couple, or family client with an identified alcohol problem.

Identification and Intervention of Alcohol Problems

Initial Decision-making
Once you become aware that drinking is a problem for a family, you must ask yourself a series of questions:

1. What type of drinking problem does this family have and how severe and acute is it?
2. Should I address the drinking problem at all? If so, when should I do so?
3. If I address the drinking, to what degree will I be able to help the family?
4. Should I involve the drinker or other family members in alcohol-specific specialty services instead of, or in addition to, the treatment that I provide?
5. If I take some of the responsibility for addressing the drinking, should I work only with the drinker for a while, or should I also continue working with other family members?
6. If I do continue working with the family, to what extent should the children be involved?

There are some initial decisions you will need to make before proceeding with any intervention:

Determine the Type and Severity of the Alcohol Problem:
      Family alcohol problems can range in severity from conflicts about what is

considered acceptable drinking behavior to severe alcohol dependence with resulting physical dependence or medical problems.

More severe problems will require immediate, specialized attention; those that are less severe can be addressed in the context of the overall treatment plan.

Decide Whether Identified Drinking Problems Should Be Addressed or NOT:
Although it might seem counter-intuitive to **ignore** an important problem, there may be reasons for doing so. (1) Treatment may be directed to another severe or acute problem, such as child abuse or the terminal illness of a family member. (2) You may have a limited number of sessions or limited time during which the family is available for treatment. (3) You may be concerned that any discussion of drinking problems will result in the termination of treatment. Although this outcome is uncommon when drinking issues are raised in a respectful, client-centered manner (as described later in this, you may choose to postpone a direct discussion of drinking if you are convinced that it would cause the family to leave treatment.

If you have decided to address it, then: (1) Determine whether the drinking is related to the presenting problem - either directly or indirectly. (2) Determine the severity of the alcohol problem, and in some cases, provide a diagnosis. (3) Obtain a detailed picture of the cognitive, affective, and motivational aspects of the drinking behavior. (4) Collect information that will form the basis of feedback to the drinker and/or the drinker's family. (5) Determine which of the available treatment options is most appropriate.

Guide decision-making related to the treatment plan. Three essential domains that any alcohol assessment should cover are: (1) level and pattern of alcohol use; (2) dependence symptoms; and the severity of the problem; and (3) consequences of alcohol use.

Screening and Problem Assessment

Given the prevalence of drinking problems and the serious consequences that can result, brief screening procedures should be used routinely in your clinical practice to identify individuals who are experiencing or are at risk for experiencing alcohol problems. Before making any treatment decisions, a multi-dimensional problem assessment, which covers alcohol use patterns, dependence signs and symptoms, and alcohol consequences should be performed.

The tools normally used for screening and assessment are flexible enough to be used with adults in individual, couple, or family therapy contexts. At times, you will be required to screen and assess alcohol use in adolescents, and even 'kids' i.e., under 12, but such assessment should be done by therapists who are versed in dealing with adolescent and childhood problems. Normally these cases would be treated first at psychological issues, rather than alcohol issues first.

For information on the assessment and diagnosis of alcohol use disorders in adolescents, there are many resources on line, and research niaa.nih.gov publications.

For assessment, "Drinking Self-Monitoring Logs" are an excellent tool. Daily records tend to eliminate much of the bias associated with retrospective recall. However, they are often kept during a narrow window of time (e.g., 2 weeks) because of practical limitations, and therefore may not be representative of the drinker's typical drinking behavior. A major strength of log reporting is that it may be used simultaneously to assess contextual information related to the respondent's drinking occasions (e.g., time, place, mood, interpersonal context), which can be useful in treatment planning.

Therapy or counseling "Prompted Daily Recall and Timeline Methods" are subject to the client's honesty and denial. They can often conveniently forget some of their drinking, or as one of my clients does, he considers drinking champagne not part of his alcoholism, and only counts hard liquor! These methods use prompts, calendars, or charts to collect recalled drinking behavior on specific dates or days of the week. During this evaluation, the drinker generally is asked to estimate the number of drinking hours, which can provide critical information for accurately estimating highest Blood Alcohol Levels (BALs) achieved. Timeline methods have been shown to yield pretty reliable estimates of drinking behavior.

Assessing Dependence Symptoms and Severity of the Problem

Assessing dependence symptoms is critical to determining the appropriate treatment option.

Two self-report instruments typically used are:
The 25-item **Alcohol Dependence Scale** (ADS) and the 20-item **Severity of Alcohol**

Dependence Questionnaire (SADQ). Both are available in the Appendix.

If you wish to make a formal diagnosis, or if you want detailed data related to a differential diagnosis (e.g., alcohol abuse vs. alcohol dependence), structured and semi-structured diagnostic interviews are recommended. Even if your goal is not to make a formal diagnosis, diagnostic instruments such as the two listed below, provide excellent questions to guide your assessment interview:

- The Alcohol Use Disorders and Associated Disabilities Interview Schedule (AUDADIS).
- The Structured Clinical Interview for DSM-IV (SCID).

Study Questions

13. The field of family therapy has developed a number of theoretical concepts and techniques that can help substance abuse treatment providers better understand clients' relationships with their families. One such technique refers to an interactional pattern in which members of an intimate relationship establish roles and take on behavioral patterns that fulfill the unconscious needs and demands of the other. This technique is called:

    a. Intervention
    b. Complementarity
    c. MSMC Karaoke Night
    d. Recidivism

14. Family rules and scripts are NOT unchangeable, but families exhibit different degrees of adaptability when faced with the need to change patterns of behavior. There is a tendency in all families to achieve a state of equilibrium that balances strong, competing forces in families as they tend to resist change. This must be overcome if change is to occur. What is this called?

    a. homeostasis
    b. homeopathy
    c. homeboy
    d. homosexual
    e. halitosis

15. In order to function well, families need to be able to preserve order and stability without becoming too rigid to adapt.

    True   False

16. What is it called when two family members need to discuss a sensitive issue but instead of facing the issue, they divert their energy to a third person/member who acts as a go-between, scapegoat, object of concern, or ally. By involving this other person, they reduce their emotional tension, but prevent their conflict from being resolved and miss opportunities to increase the intimacy in their relationship.

    a. Abstinence
    b. enmeshment
    c. triangulation.
    d. disengagement
    e. none of the above

17. Integrated treatment includes differing Levels of Involvement with Families. Substance abuse treatment professionals intervene with families at different levels during treatment. These levels vary according to:

    a. how individualized the interventions are to each family
    b. the extent to which the substance abuse treatment provider is trained and supervised in family therapy techniques
    c. the extent to which family therapy is integrated into the process of substance abuse treatment.
    d. all of the above
    e. none of the above

18. Name some integrated treatment models, and explain how two work.

19. What are the THREE stages of sobriety?

20. There are THREE stages of sobriety, and how families cope at different points in the progression of treatment. Which of the following is the proper order?

    a. Long-Term Maintenance of Sobriety: The family must re-balance and stabilize a new and healthier lifestyle. Attainment of Sobriety: The family system is unbalanced but healthy change is possible. Adjustment to Sobriety:

The family works on developing and stabilizing a new system.

b. Attainment of Sobriety: The family system is unbalanced but healthy change is possible. Adjustment to Sobriety: The family works on developing and stabilizing a new system. Long-Term Maintenance of Sobriety: The family must re-balance and stabilize a new and healthier lifestyle.

c. Long-Term Maintenance of Sobriety: The family must re-balance and stabilize a new and healthier lifestyle. Adjustment to Sobriety: The family works on developing and stabilizing a new system. Attainment of Sobriety: The family system is unbalanced but healthy change is possible.

d. Attainment of Sobriety: The family system is unbalanced but healthy change is possible. Adjustment to Sobriety: The family works on developing and stabilizing a new system. Relapse from Sobriety: The family must re-balance and stabilize to a the recidivism and hope for a new awakening.

21. What are some of the things needed to maintain sobriety?

22. If the client is seeing you for Substance Abuse issues, why would you want to evaluate them for Domestic or Child Abuse?

23. The feeling or emotion, especially as manifested by facial expression or body language:

    a. disengagement
    b. effect
    c. triangulation
    d. affect

Notes:

UNIT 7

Alcohol Problems Framework

Alcohol Problems Framework

Since the 1930s, "alcoholics" have been the primary focus of substance abuse related intervention efforts in the United States. While a focus on severe problems is typical of an initial societal response to a health problem, alcohol dependence represents only a small portion of the entire range of alcohol-related problems.

Most drinking problems are of mild to moderate severity and are amenable to relatively brief interventions. In a report to the National Institute on Alcohol Abuse and Alcoholism (NIAAA), the Institute of Medicine (IOM)4 called for a "broadening of the base for treatment" and widespread adoption of an alcohol problems framework. This framework casts a wide net for treatment efforts, explicitly targeting individuals (or families) who currently are experiencing or are at risk for experiencing alcohol problems. Thus, therapists and health care professionals are asked to direct interventions not only to drinkers with alcohol use disorders, but also to problem drinkers and "at-risk" drinkers.

Even small amounts of alcohol consumed during pregnancy, or in combination with certain medications, may result in significant adverse consequences and therefore constitute risky drinking. Population estimates for alcohol use disorders do not include the millions of adults who experience less severe alcohol-related problems or who engage in risky drinking patterns that could potentially lead to problems. Criteria for alcohol use disorders are relatively clear, but establishing a "cut-off point" to separate problem drinkers from non-problem drinkers is difficult, making population estimates more problematic.

Although a pattern of recurrent trouble related to alcohol may indicate a more serious alcohol problem, experiencing any alcohol related problem is cause for concern. A recent national study found that approximately 21% of Americans experienced at least one alcohol-related problem in the prior year, and roughly one in three Americans engaged in risky drinking patterns.

These base rates for alcohol problems and risky drinking are high in the general population, but they are considerably higher in clinical populations. Given the high rates of co-morbidity between alcohol use disorders and other psychiatric disorders, and the strong association that exists between drinking behavior and mood regulation, stress, and interpersonal and family problems, a high proportion of individuals, couples, and families who present for therapy may be experiencing or may be at risk for alcohol problems.

Alcohol Problems: Identification and Intervention

I - Implications for Intervention

The alcohol problems framework explicitly recognizes tremendous heterogeneity in the severity, duration, progression, etiology, consequences, and manifestations of alcohol problems. If you wish to address alcohol problems in your individual, marital, or family practice, this heterogeneity requires that you are equipped with:

1. A means to identify individuals with alcohol problems or those at risk for problems.
2. Procedures for further assessment to determine the nature and severity of the problem, and to guide treatment decisions.
3. Knowledge of a range of educational and clinical interventions that can be matched to the nature and severity of the problem.

II - Alcohol Use Disorders

The Diagnostic and Statistical Manual of Mental Disorders, Fourth Edition Revised (DSM-IVR), and recent update DSM-V, recognize two alcohol use disorders: alcohol dependence and alcohol abuse.

Alcohol dependence is characterized by multiple symptoms, including tolerance, signs of withdrawal, diminished control over drinking, as well as cognitive, behavioral, and/or physiological symptoms that suggest the individual continues to drink despite experiencing significant alcohol-related problems.

Alcohol abuse is a maladaptive pattern of drinking that leads to clinically significant impairment or distress. An individual diagnosed with alcohol abuse drinks despite alcohol-related physical, social, psychological, or occupational problems. Alcohol abuse does not necessarily entail a consistent pattern of heavy drinking, but is defined by the adverse consequences associated with the drinking pattern.

III - Problem Drinking and Risky Drinking

As it is commonly used, "problem drinking" often is synonymous with "alcoholism." Among professionals, however, increasingly it is used to describe non-dependent drinking that results in adverse consequences for the drinker.

In contrast to the dependent drinker, the problem drinker's alcohol problems do not stem from compulsive alcohol seeking, but often are the direct result of intoxication. Problem drinking Alcohol Problems represents a broader category than alcohol abuse disorder. The problem drinker may or may not have a problem severe enough to meet criteria for alcohol abuse disorder. While problem drinkers are currently experiencing adverse consequences as a result of drinking, risky drinkers consume alcohol in a pattern that puts them at risk for these adverse consequences. Risky drinking patterns include high-volume drinking, high-quantity consumption on any given day, and even any consumption, if various medical or situational factors are present.

Alcohol Consumption is quantified in terms of standard drinks, which contain approximately 14 grams, or .6 fluid ounces, of pure alcohol.

Risky drinking can be determined by identifying one or more of the patterns below:

High-volume drinking: 14 or more standard drinks per week on average for males, and seven or more standard drinks for females.

High-quantity consumption: Consumption on any given day of 5 or more standard drinks for males, and four or more standard drinks for females.

Any consumption within certain contexts: Even when small quantities of alcohol are ingested, drinking is risky if it occurs within contexts that pose a particular danger, for example, during pregnancy, when certain health conditions are present, when certain medications are taken, etc.

IV - The Continuum of Alcohol Problems

Alcohol problems can range in severity from mild, negative consequences in a single life situation to severe alcohol dependence with significant medical, employment, and interpersonal consequences. As shown in Figure 1, alcohol use and its associated problems can be viewed on a continuum - ranging from no alcohol problems following modest consumption, to severe problems often associated with heavy consumption.

V - The Prevalence of Problems

Alcohol abuse and alcohol dependence are among the most prevalent mental disorders in the United States. In 1992, 7.4% of U.S. adults aged 18 years and older - roughly 14 million Americans - were found to have an alcohol use disorder - alcohol dependence or abuse.

———————————————

Study Questions

24. The primary factor distinguishing alcohol dependence from other alcohol problems.
    a. Tolerance
    b. Risky drinking
    c. Role impairment
    d. Family dysfunction

25. According to the article, approximately 1 in ? Americans engaged in risky drinking patterns within the previous year.
    a. 2
    b. 3
    c. 5
    d. 9

26. A family problem/s that are likely to co-occur with alcohol use disorders.
    a. Violence
    b. Infidelity
    c. Economic insecurity
    d. All of the above

27. According to the text, alcohol treatment decisions should be based on a multi-dimensional assessment that includes all of the following except:
    a. Consequences
    b. Dependence signs
    c. Biological background
    d. Use patterns

28. Unless the presenting problem is substance abuse related, all potential therapy clients should be screened for substance abuse related problems. (Why?)
    True   False

Level and Pattern of Alcohol Use

Although our overview is limited to a review of assessment strategies and instruments related specifically to alcohol problems, a broader assessment that covers other areas of psychological and interpersonal functioning is recommended prior to clinical intervention. Clinician skill and preference, as well as client literacy, will determine whether self-report instruments or interviews are selected.

There are three major types of methods for assessing consumption, each of which has particular strengths and weaknesses:

Self-reports of the frequency and **quantity of recent alcohol** use remain the most reliable indicators of alcohol consumption patterns available. However, if the person is intoxicated at the time of assessment or has a severe drinking problem, consumption measures may not be accurate and should be corroborated with other markers of drinking behavior, such as biomedical markers or collateral (e.g., a spouse) reports.

Quantity-Frequency (Q-F) Methods. Standard questions about how much and how often someone drinks yield typical frequency (number of days drinking), typical quantity (amount consumed), and derived from these, a quantity-frequency index representing the average amount of alcohol consumed in a specified time period. One advantage of this type of assessment is its brevity.

Notes:

UNIT 8

Intervention

Consequences of Alcohol Use

Drinking consequences represent a domain independent of dependence symptoms and should be measured separately. While many screening instruments and diagnostic clinical interviews contain Alcohol Problems: Identification and Intervention interview questions designed to identify negative consequences, having your clients complete a self-administered questionnaire will provide a detailed picture of negative consequences across a variety of life domains, and in the case of marital or family assessment, from different family member perspectives.

A thorough assessment of consequences also can be useful when evaluating treatment effects, since these measures have been shown to be sensitive to changes in drinking-related problems over time. Communicating these assessment results often is useful in helping the drinker appreciate the connection between drinking and negative consequences across life domains.

When deciding on the type of intervention, and type of counseling, The Drinker Inventory of Consequences (DrInC), the full 50-item checklist of potentially adverse drinking consequences provides summary scores in five areas and is useful in making the decision: Interpersonal; Physical; Social; Impulsive; Intrapersonal.

The full DrInC generally takes less than 10 minutes to complete. For the purposes of the class, the questions can be and should be used as a guide for discussions with the client and used to help you decide what tactics you will use. The shorter 35 item DrInC is available in the Appendix.

Decide on the Timing of Your Response

Respond immediately if drinking is causing acute medical, psychological, or interpersonal problems and refer for acute services.

With less acute problems, consider the goals set and progress made within treatment and how a discussion of drinking may influence the achievement of those goals. If the therapeutic situation is tenuous, a direct discussion of drinking problems might strengthen the alliance by bringing a major hidden issue into the open. Conversely, addressing the drinking habits of one family member may undermine an already tenuous alliance.

Drinking may underpin the presenting problems, such as a couple's concerns with finances, sexual functioning, or allocation of time. Child or spousal abuse also may be linked directly to one family member's drinking. When drinking is closely tied to presenting problems, you should address the drinking early in the treatment.

Drinking may be addressed directly and more immediately if it is interfering with achieving treatment goals, such as lack of follow-through on homework assignments, erratic attendance, or other types of interference.

If drinking appears to be more marginally related to presenting problems and treatment is progressing smoothly, it can be addressed later in treatment.

Decide Whether to Treat Alcohol Problems within Family Treatment or Through Referral, at least two elements will contribute to this decision:
1. The centrality of drinking to presenting family problems. If drinking is linked directly to presenting problems, you probably cannot proceed successfully with treatment unless drinking issues are incorporated into the treatment plan.
2. Your own expertise and comfort level in managing drinking-related problems. If you have some level of knowledge and expertise, integrating drinking issues into the larger treatment plan may be effective. If you have less expertise, you may feel more comfortable with adjunctive treatment that directly addresses the drinking and that allows you to facilitate and support the adjunctive treatment.

Brief Interventions

Decide Whether to See the Entire Family or Just the Drinker

If drinking is central to a family's problems, and you decide to intervene, it may be necessary to put aside other aspects of the family therapy until the drinking problem is stabilized and changes have been initiated. You may see the individual family member with the identified drinking problem alone for a period of time, and then bring other family members back into treatment.

64

Decide Whether to Involve the Children

There are several positive reasons for involving the children: Children typically are acutely aware if a parent is drinking heavily. Discussing the drinking with the children present brings what may have been a taboo topic out into the open.

Even young children are aware that alcohol is a unique, special beverage and can link parental drinking to changes in behavior. The children's presence during treatment may give you opportunities to educate them about drinking, and to reassure them that a problem previously hidden in the family can now be discussed. Involving children in treatment sessions may also present drawbacks:

Boundary issues between parents and children may be violated in destructive ways by a full discussion of drinking issues with the children present. For example, it is common for intimate partners to be sharply divided and to have strong negative affect around drinking. Opportunities to learn to discuss, resolve, or manage these negative emotions may be provided more effectively without the children present.

Any extensive discussion of drinking problems will involve addressing other personal problems and intimate couples issues that may be inappropriate for children to hear. If there is violence in the family, it might not be safe to ask children to discuss their parent's drinking.

Raising Drinking Issues in the Context of Family Therapy

There are no simple answers to the clinical decisions outlined above. If you decide to bring drinking problems into the therapeutic session, the next challenge is to determine how you can raise drinking issues and facilitate the family's acceptance of drinking as a legitimate part of the therapeutic agenda.

It is important to link drinking to the presenting family concerns or Alcohol Problems. The use of three major therapeutic principles: empathy; motivation through attention to client goals; and choice can facilitate the successful introduction of drinking issues into therapy.

Some General Therapeutic Principles

Accurate Empathy is strongly associated with a positive response to treatment for drinking problems. This is the place where self-disclosure can be some help when a counselor has experienced their own recovery. However, an empathetic counselor can succeed even if they have not been abusers themselves.

Traditional approaches to alcohol treatment have taken a more confrontational style in which attempts are made to "break through" client denial to facilitate awareness of the extent and severity of their drinking. Research, however, does not support this approach. Instead, it finds that clinicians who can understand the complex emotions clients experience concerning his/her drinking and who can communicate this understanding in an empathic and supportive manner are more likely to achieve success in enabling clients to:
1. Discuss their drinking
2. Realize the problems associated with it
3. Prepare to change. From the first moment that you address drinking, utilizing an empathic approach is crucial.

Enhance Motivation by Focusing on Client Goals

Traditional views of change in drinking habits held that motivation was a trait that a client either did or did not have. Life experience, not clinician or family action, was the vehicle by which motivation would lead to change. However, contemporary research contradicts this traditional view. It offers substantial evidence that you can enhance your clients' motivation to change by using specific therapeutic behaviors, and by providing family members with interventions to change their behavior as well.

You can enhance client motivation by linking the client's drinking to their own positive goals. In particular, if there is a discrepancy between the client's current life circumstance and the specific goals that he/she has articulated, drinking may be contributing to this discrepancy between goals and desires.

Helping the client make this linkage can provide a powerful source of motivation to change. Give Client Choices. Providing clients who have drinking problems with choices about how to select treatment options and how to articulate treatment goals will result in better treatment retention and more positive outcomes.

Instead of assuming an authoritative stance that directs the drinker to one course of action, you can provide choices that help the drinker to become knowledgeable about these options. You also can provide guidance about the advantages and disadvantages of various options without trying to force the client to select a specific choice.

Applying the General Principles

How can you use the three principles to successfully introduce drinking issues into family therapy?

Any discussion of drinking should be approached with an **Empathic and Respectful Demeanor**. You might introduce the topic by saying: "I'd like to bring up a topic that we haven't talked about too much," or "I've been thinking about another issue that might be contributing to the difficulties that you've been having," or "It might be important to talk a bit more about how alcohol fits into the problems you've been experiencing. I've gotten the sense that this might be an uncomfortable topic."

Each of these introductions is intended to be low-key, gentle, and non-accusatory in tone, reflecting your awareness that the drinker and other family members might find the topic difficult to address.

After an initial introduction, you may respond to each client with reflective listening comments. In this example, the therapist expresses empathy without taking sides:

Therapist: "It might be important to talk a bit more about how alcohol fits into the problems you've been experiencing. I've gotten the sense that this might be an uncomfortable topic."

Husband: "I knew it would come to this. My wife has been blaming everything on my drinking for years, and she promised she wouldn't bring it up here. I wouldn't have come to see you if I thought we'd be back on that old train again."

Therapist: "So you're feeling set up now, and kind of angry that I'm bringing up the same topic?"

Link Drinking to Client Goals and Aspirations. In family therapy, applying this principle is relatively easy. Clients seeking family therapy typically have a set of concerns that motivated them to seek assistance:

Brief Interventions
Communication

67

Decision-making
Intimacy
Finances
Sexual incompatibility
Management of family responsibilities
Child behavior problems
Parenting

If one person is drinking heavily, that drinking is likely to be contributing to the family's presenting problems. Your challenge is to understand how the drinking may be playing a role in the presenting problems, and to articulate this understanding to the family.

For example: **Therapist**: "Although I am hearing, loud and clear, that you don't want to talk about your drinking, I am concerned that it may somehow be connected with the concerns the two of you came in with. You both said that you wanted help in becoming better parents, and that you were having too many arguments about discipline and rules. From what you've been telling me, I have a hunch that the different feelings you each have about John's drinking and his time away from the house may be affecting your ability to come to agreement about rules for your kids."

Even if drinking is not centrally related to the problems that brought a family into treatment, one family member's drinking might be creating barriers to successful progress in treatment. You may explain that you are raising drinking as an issue because of problems encountered in progressing in treatment.

Non-compliance with homework assignments, observing that specific types of assignments fall apart (e.g., having a couple go out together, or discuss a problem during the evening), or feeling bewildered about aspects of a family's functioning, are all clues that the drinking might be a contributing factor. Feedback about the linkages between drinking and lack of progress in treatment also can be used to introduce the topic of alcohol into therapy.

Applying Principles of Choice

The principle of **choice** becomes prominent as alcohol issues are explored more fully, but even in the initial discussion, you must keep this principle in mind. After first discussing drinking, you can give the family a choice about the degree to which the topic is pursued in any one session. You also can be clear that discussing drinking is not equivalent to requiring that anyone change their behavior, and that the family will be involved actively in decision-making about how to proceed.

Some Common Pitfalls

Although normally it ultimately will be constructive and valuable to address drinking in the context of marital or family therapy, you must be prepared for pitfalls that are unique to the marital/family therapy context:

Defensiveness On the Part of the Drinker - Expect to hear assertions that the drinking is not a problem, is under control, can be controlled whenever the drinker desires, or that others are "making too big a deal about a few drinks." The three therapeutic principles that guide this section - empathy; motivation through goals; and choices - are all intended to attenuate the drinker's defensive reactions.

Reactions of Other Family Members During Any Discussion of Drinking - Family members may experience relief that the topic is being addressed, and may make strong efforts to ally with you against the family member with the problem drinking. Such comments as, "I've been concerned about that too," or "She's right, we have to face this," are hints that a family member is trying to become your ally against the drinker. You must make efforts to neutralize the alliance, i.e., maintain an alliance with the family as a unit, rather than with specific family members.

Negative Reactions by Family Members to Your Empathic Responses to the Drinker - Family members, who often have experienced anger, frustration, fear, and sadness in response to years of problem drinking, may be impatient to see change occur once the topic of drinking is introduced into therapy. They may hope that you will "straighten out" the drinker, providing definitive instructions to stop the drinking behavior and to seek a specific form of treatment. When you do not respond accordingly, family members may react negatively. They may become angry with you for expressing empathy about how difficult it is to face and change a drinking problem, or for trying to help the client make decisions about how, when, and how much to change. You must walk a careful line, not sacrificing the needs or desires of any family member to those of others in the family. A balanced, empathic, and respectful response to the reactions of each family member can neutralize some of the intense emotions that surround this topic.

Family Members May Develop Alliance Against You - As a reflection of their desire to avoid discussing the role of alcohol in their family or the problems it has caused, the family may develop an alliance against you. Different factors may lead to a family alliance to avoid any discussion of drinking, including:

- Family lack of understanding about, or prejudice towards, alcohol use disorders.
- Family embarrassment or shame.
- Family members' concern that their own drinking behavior might also be challenged or affected.
- Family homeostatic balance that is threatened by any discussion of drinking.

Your response to family level resistance will be determined, at least in part, by your understanding of why the family is resisting the need to address drinking. However, it is not advocated to a doggedly pursue the issue of drinking to the extent that the family drops out of treatment. It is a measured approach that integrates drinking issues into a larger case formulation and treatment plan for the entire family.

Elements of Brief Interventions

When the Drinker Is Present

The success of brief interventions for drinking problems is well supported by research conducted over the past 25 years. The approach described below, best characterized as adapted motivational interviewing, can be an effective treatment for some alcohol use disorders without the need for further clinical intervention. It also may resolve mild to moderate alcohol problems, enhance the client's readiness to address more severe drinking problems, and result in acceptance of a treatment referral.

Major elements of the brief intervention include:
- Careful assessment of the drinking and its consequences
- Feedback
- Drinker choices
- Emphasis on personal responsibility
- Involvement of the family
- Follow-up

You should deliver all six elements of the brief intervention using a motivational

70

interviewing style. The six principles and techniques that guide brief interventions.

Assessment

For the brief intervention, you should obtain information that will help the drinker and other family members understand why and in what ways their drinking is problematic. Several types of information, which can be obtained using questionnaires and interview questions, are helpful in achieving this understanding.

Feedback

A key element in brief interventions is the feedback provided to the drinker. A major purpose of feedback is to help the drinker recognize discrepancies that exist between his/her current circumstances and personal and family goals and aspirations. Feedback should be conveyed in a warm, empathic tone, and should be descriptive rather than evaluative. The clinician may introduce the feedback by saying:

To the drinker: "We've been spending a bit of time discussing your drinking, and you also spent some time filling out questionnaires that I gave you. I'd like to offer some feedback on what I've learned about your drinking, and what I think it suggests. Please feel free to ask questions as I go along. Then we can talk about your reactions and thoughts."

To the family: "You'll probably find this interesting as well, and you may want to comment. Feel free to ask questions, but I suggest that you hold other comments until we've had some time to go through all the feedback."

Feedback can be organized on a feedback sheet for the family to review. A feedback form should include:

Feedback about Drinking Habits, i.e., the average number of standard drinks consumed each week. A standard drink is equal to one 12-ounce beer, one 5-ounce glass of table wine, one 3-ounce glass of fortified wine, or a 1.5-ounce shot of hard liquor.

Average number of drinks ingested on each drinking day. Calculate this number by adding together the total number of drinks consumed, and divide by the number of days the client drank.

Highest consumption. Look at all the drinking information and write in the largest amount the client drank on any given day.

A Sample Feedback Sheet to fill in and give to the family would be something like this:

---

1. Based on the information I obtained during the assessment sessions, I calculated the number of "standard drinks" you consumed each day.
     I have summarized three important indicators of your drinking:
_____ Total number of standard drinks per week.
_____ Average number of standard drinks per drinking day.
_____ Highest consumption in a day.

2. When we look at everyone who drinks in the United States, you have been drinking more than approximately _____ percent of the population of women/men in the country. I also estimated your highest and average blood alcohol level (BAL) in the past month. Your BAL is based on how many standard drinks you consume, the length of time over which you drink that much, whether you are a man or a woman, and how much you weigh.

Your estimated peak BAL in an average week was _____.
Your estimated average BAL in an average week was _____.

This is a measure of how intoxicated you typically become. In the U.S. the legal intoxication limit is .08 or .10 (confirm the BAL limit for your specific state).

3. You have experienced negative consequences from drinking. Here are some of the most important of those consequences:
a.
b.
c.
Please understand that this information is based on what I have gathered in our sessions from you, and from your family.

To make a comparison of drinking to national norms, you can refer to a standardized chart available on the internet to determine where your client's drinking falls. For example, a man who drinks 28 drinks per week is at the 90th percentile - 90% of men in the U.S. drink less than he does. Such feedback is valuable because many heavy drinkers associate with other heavy drinkers and believe that their own drinking pattern is "normal" rather than heavy.

Blood alcohol level (BAL)

To determine BAL, the clinician weighs four factors: amount consumed; time over which alcohol is consumed; client body weight; and client sex. Use of standard BAL charts (again available on the internet) yields information on usual BAL as well as the BAL achieved on the heaviest drinking days. Comparing the BAL calculated to the legally defined limit for intoxicated driving in the client's state of residence (typically .08 or .10) provides a context in which to understand the client's BAL.

Feedback About Negative Consequences of Drinking

Information about negative consequences has been provided already by the drinker and other family members, but summarizing negative consequences often has a notable impact. The clinician can organize this section into:
Subjective negative consequences.
Objective negative consequences.
Concerns of the family not necessarily shared by the drinker.
Links between the drinking and either presenting family problems, or problems with progressing in therapy.

After the Feedback

At the conclusion of the feedback session, client and family reactions will vary widely: They may be moved emotionally, reacting to the feedback with sadness or shame; they may objectify the information and ask factually oriented questions; they may react neutrally, disagree, or minimize the significance of the information; they may interpret it as a signal to take action; the family members may become angry with the drinker and attempt to chastise, lecture, or express long-held negative feelings.

Keep in mind that the goal of feedback is to enhance the drinker's willingness to make changes in his/her drinking. Continue using the skills of motivational interviewing by: taking an empathic stance; avoiding the urge to confront resistance; eliciting reactions from the drinker and family members; acknowledging and respecting the complex reactions all members of the family might have; and supporting statements that suggest the drinker is considering change.

Choice

After discussing reactions of the drinker and family members to the feedback, the conversation should move to determining possible next steps. Here, it is important to ensure that the drinker has choices and does not feel forced to select one option. Any movement toward change should be considered a positive outcome of the brief intervention.

Although total abstinence from alcohol is always a safe, desirable outcome, reductions in drinking can lead to improved health and social functioning. Reductions in drinking also may serve as a way station to abstinence, whereby the drinker attempts to cut down, and ultimately decides that abstinence is either an easier choice or a necessary one.

Although some drinkers may ask for specific advice and information about available treatments, many may respond by stating that they accept the need for change but want to try to change on their own. Both treatment and self-change can lead to positive results, so you can support either plan.

Providing a drinker with choices is more than passive acceptance of the individual's goals and preferred route to change. You can play an active role by providing specific information about different goals and different treatment options. Lay out your view of the advantages and disadvantages of each option, and even suggest a preferred course of action. Having an educational discussion and clearly stating the importance of choosing a route to change that is acceptable will enhance the likelihood of success.

Although the main target of this discussion is the drinker, the other family members should be encouraged to express their views about advantages and disadvantages of different approaches. By the end of the discussion, the ideal outcome invokes a specific change plan. Referral for specialty treatment; involvement with self-help; continued work on the drinking in the family therapy; or an initial attempt at self-change are all acceptable change plans. If the drinker is not willing to commit to any plan, you should respect that choice, but indicate that you will return to a discussion

74

of drinking in future sessions after the entire family has had the opportunity to think about the feedback.

Use of Motivational Interviewing Style

Motivational interviewing is an empathetic, client-centered, therapeutic style and should be used when conducting brief interventions. Three major principles underpin motivational interviewing:

Express Empathy: Empathy implies an acceptance of each family member's experience, perspectives, and emotions, and requires the ability to express this acceptance in a warm, compassionate manner. The use of active reflective listening is key.

Roll With Resistance: Drinkers often attempt to persuade others that their drinking is not problematic. Such an argument tends to solidify the drinker's viewpoint. If you avoid arguments, empathically accept that the drinker is ambivalent, and encourage the drinker to merely consider an alternative viewpoint, resistance is likely to decrease.

When the Drinker Is Present Enhance and Support Self-efficacy: You should view the drinker as capable of changing and communicate that perspective in a number of ways: Note the drinker's strengths (e.g., commitment to family, success in the work place); Communicate respect for the serious manner in which the drinker is responding to the brief intervention;   Provide general information about the success drinkers tend to have in changing their behavior over time; Help the drinker to envision himself/herself as a person who can change and to realize the importance of making the decision to change.

_____

Study Questions

29. Primary goals of alcohol assessment include all the following, except:
    a. Determine whether the drinking is related to the presenting.
    b. Determine the severity of the alcohol problem.
    c. Collect information that will form the basis of feedback.
    d. Determine if the drinking has a genetic foundation.

30. To make a diagnosis or differential diagnosis, the recommended method of data collection is:
    a. The 25-item Alcohol Dependence Scale (ADS)
    b. The 20-item Severity of Alcohol Dependence Questionnaire

c. Structured and semi-structured diagnostic interviews
d. None of the above

31. A tool that should be considered for obtaining and/or tracking changes in data to drinking consequences.
      a. The Drinker Inventory of Consequences (DrInC)
      b. The Drinking Consequences Inventory - Revised (DCI-R)
      c. The Rascal-III Self-report Inventory
      d. All of the above

32. Primary goals of substance abuse treatment include eliminating substance abuse as a factor in the following areas of functioning, except:
      a. Social
      b. Occupational
      c. Physical
      d. Psychological

33. Mild to moderate problem drinking should usually be treated with a brief intervention protocol.
      True   False

34. Which of the following would be the most effective therapy method to treat mild to moderate drinking problems:
      a. Gestalt
      b. Reichian
      c. Jared's Juice Purge
      d. Cognitive Behavioral Therapy
      e. Jungian

35. Reasons not to immediately address a drinking problem might include:
      a. A limited number of sessions available.
      b. Need to address more acute behaviors first (e.g. Child abuse, suicidality).
      c. Concern that addressing initially may cause termination of therapy.
      d. All of the above.

36. If a patient presents with immediate medical, psychological, or interpersonal problems, the recommended treatment option would be:
      a. Refer to acute care.
      b. Add community base self-help to treatment approach.
      c. Conduct more in depth assessment over next 2 sessions.

d. Assign appropriate bibliotherapy.

37. A reason not to involve children in substance abuse related family intervention:
    a. It is a family secret that should be handled at home.
    b. Concern for safety of child speaking out if there is a history of violence.
    c. May provide children with education regarding drinking behaviors.
    d. Young children are unable to link behavioral changes with substance abuse.

38. For most, motivation to quit drinking is either present or not and cannot be enhanced.
    True   False

39. When introducing drinking as an issue, it is important to include the following:
    a. Empathy to both drinker and family.
    b. Focus on client and family goals.
    c. Client choices
    d. All of the above

40. It is usually beneficial to introduce the topic of problem drinking in family therapy assertively and with authority.
    True   False

41. Which of the following is NOT a suggested way to introduce the topic of problem drinking in family therapy?
    a. assertively and with authority
    b. empathetically and respectfully
    c. gently and non-accusatory
    d. low-key and reflectively)

42. Not mentioned as a pitfall to addressing substance abuse problems in the context of family therapy:
    a. The entire family may build an alliance against the therapist.
    b. The abuser may accept responsibility removing the family roles of others.
    c. Negative reactions by non-problem drinking family members to empathy.
    d. All of the above were mentioned as pitfalls.

43. Use of the _____ interviewing style is recommended in addressing drinking.
    a. Motivational
    b. CBT based short screen
    c. Self-centered

d. Semi-unstructured

Notes:

UNIT 9

Intervention II

Personal Responsibility

Whether an individual chooses to initiate change in their own behavior ultimately is their responsibility. During the brief intervention, you should communicate this principle clearly to the drinker and to the family members. Families can help and support a person in their change efforts, and may serve as a source of motivation for change, but the ultimate decision is an individual one.

You can communicate this principle through comments such as:
"It is your decision to do what you want to do," "I appreciate that this is a lot of information and that you might want to think about it more before reacting," or
[To the family]: "I know that you're eager for John to stop drinking, but he has to feel comfortable with that kind of decision and know that it's the right thing for him to do."

At the same time, family members have the right to make choices for which they will be responsible. A spouse may decide that living in a relationship with someone who is drinking daily or heavily is not acceptable, and may choose to separate from the drinker who continues to drink. Such a decision requires an acceptance of responsibility, rather than focusing on the drinker's responsibility (e.g., "I will choose to leave if you keep drinking," versus "You made me leave because you wouldn't stop drinking.")

Family Involvement

We have mentioned some of the potential family's reactions during the brief intervention. Here are some a\Additional roles the family may play include:

Providing Additional Feedback to the Drinker: This may include feedback about negative consequences resulting from drinking, or objectionable behaviors observed when drinking; the results of previous change attempts; or family members' subjective reactions to the drinking or to the clinician's feedback. Encouraging the use of constructive communication skills is key to successful family feedback. Suggest that they use "I" statements rather than attacks, and expressions of care and concern rather than expressions of blame or contempt.

Supporting the Drinker's Attempts to Change: This is a topic that may continue through future sessions, but which can be introduced during the brief intervention. As the drinker decides upon a course of action, you may ask the family to consider ways to support these actions.

Finding Ways to Support and Reinforce Positive Change: Families might spend more time with the drinker when abstinent, express positive reactions to changes in drinking (e.g., "I really enjoyed today), or provide positive feedback through concrete actions (e.g., a heartfelt hug.)

Stating Specific Limits: Family members may have decided on limits about what they will tolerate, and what they plan to do should the drinking continue unchanged. Knowledge about such limits might have an important influence on the drinker's decision-making.

Follow-up

Although most descriptions of brief interventions stop here, the family therapist who implements a brief drinking intervention usually has an on-going relationship with the family, and will have the opportunity to follow-up beyond the initial intervention.

If the drinker and family settle on a change strategy by the end of the brief intervention, you should continue to check in and monitor success and problems in future treatment sessions. If the initial plan is not succeeding, you can discuss further options.

A tone of collaboration and respect should characterize these later discussions as well. For example: "Your initial plan was to try to cut down on your own. That seemed to go quite well for a while, but lately you've been telling me that you're struggling again. Maybe we could go back to that list of options and think about whether some other option might work better for you at this point. The fact that you're interested in change and trying hard is great. Now it's a matter of finding the strategies that work best for you."

If the brief intervention does not immediately result in a change plan, you also will want to revisit the discussion in later sessions. The tone of the follow-up should continue to be respectful, and responsibility should remain with the drinker. For example: "Last week we talked quite a bit about your drinking, and you said you wanted to think about what we discussed. I'm curious to know what your thoughts have been during the week, and whether you have discussed them with your family."

Elements of Brief Interventions: When the Drinker Is Not Present

The brief intervention described earlier is designed to work directly with the drinker. However, the drinker is not always part of the treatment and may be unwilling to get involved. A second set of therapeutic strategies can help the family respond constructively to a family member's alcohol problem and motivate the drinker to change or seek treatment.

It is a myth that family members cannot influence a drinker to change. Family members cannot make an individual stop drinking, but they can change their own behavior in ways that will help the drinker recognize that the drinking is problematic, and that change is desirable. In fact, study findings support the effectiveness of such interventions.

When family members are involved in treatment without the drinker, a careful assessment is required to determine whether the affected family members are dealing with a loved one who has a drinking problem. This initial assessment should be followed up with confirmatory feedback. Providing further assessment of family coping strategies and offering guidance in specific responses form the core of such interventions. Safety issues and other aspects of self-care must also be addressed, regardless of the drinker's behavior.

Several aspects of brief interventions with the drinker not present are similar to those described previously for brief interventions with the drinker present. Others are unique to the situation where the drinker is not available to the therapist.

Assessment and Feedback about the Drinker's Drinking

Family members often are uncertain about the seriousness of the drinking of another family member. You can conduct an assessment similar to that described for the drinker using the family member's report. Ideally, you will be able to determine whether an alcohol problem is present or establish a diagnosis of alcohol abuse or dependence based on the family member's report, and also assess the quantity and frequency of drinking. After making this determination, you should give the family feedback, either to assure them that the drinking is not objectively a problem, or that it is problematic or a diagnosable disorder.

If the drinking pattern is neither problematic nor diagnosable, then your intervention should focus on discussing the different attitudes and values about drinking in the family. If the drinking is problematic, a more detailed family intervention is needed.

Assessment of Family Coping Strategies

How families cope with the drinking is an important area of assessment. Families engage in a wide range of responses to drinking, including behaviors that support or tolerate the drinking, confront or control the drinking, or attempt to withdraw from the drinking or the drinker.

You can assess family coping through interviews as well as questionnaires. In an interview, ask questions such as:
- "How have you responded to your family member's drinking?"
- "How have you tried to influence his/her drinking?"
- "How have you tried to help him/her to change?"
- "How has his/her drinking affected you?"
- "What have been some particularly difficult situations you've run into related to his/her drinking?"
- "How have you coped with these?"

Your goal is to learn how the family members have reinforced drinking, protected the drinker from experiencing negative consequences from drinking, talked with the drinker about his/her drinking behavior, and how they have been affected themselves.

There are several good questionnaires to assess family coping, including: The Coping Questionnaire; Behavior Questionnaire; Spouse Enabling Inventory; and the Spouse Sobriety Influence Inventory.

As with a drinker's assessment, an assessment of family coping should be approached in a spirit of inquiry by engaging the family in a discussion that reveals their perceptions about positive and negative actions, as well as their subjective feelings about interactions with the drinker. This assessment of family coping strategies sets the stage for suggested interventions.

Assuring Family Safety

Spouse and child abuse occur at elevated rates in families where one member has an alcohol problem. You should conduct a specific assessment for the presence of physical violence if there are drinking issues in the family. Assessment should target specific aggressive behaviors, rather than global questions such as, "Is there any violence in your home?" Specific questions should be asked about behaviors such as throwing objects, grabbing a family member roughly, slapping, pushing, hitting, or threatening harm.

Additional questions about actual injuries also should be included in the assessment. The presence of weapons in the home, particularly guns, also should be noted. If there is evidence of physical violence in the family, you must take steps to assure the safety of the family. Since some families may view such behavior as normal, it is essential that you make a clear, unambiguous statement about the need for safety and the unacceptability of being hit or otherwise hurt. Advising the family on other safety measures - such as keeping a bag packed, establishing a place to go should violence appear imminent, and understanding the role and limitations of restraining orders - also is appropriate.

If there are guns or other weapons in the home, you should consider advising either their removal or a secure locking system to prevent a potentially violent family member from accessing the weapons.

Changing Family Coping

Once you have assured the basic safety of the family, you can begin to address changes in family behavior that may help the drinker recognize his/her drinking as problematic.

Changing Consequences of Drinking

It is common for family members to try to protect the drinker from the naturally occurring negative consequences of drinking. They may assume the drinker's responsibilities; cover for the drinker at work; provide comfort and reassurance after a drinking binge; hide their feelings about the drinking; hide the drinker's problems from family or friends, etc. Each of these actions may be well intentioned, but the net effect is to shield the drinker from the consequences of absences from work, the full impact of a hangover, or the realization that a loved one is frightened or angry.

The drinker who has the opportunity to hear about such consequences gradually may realize that there is a large cost associated with drinking and may begin to consider change. You can help the family recognize the unintended adverse effects of protecting the drinker, guide them to reduce actions that protect the drinker, and help them recognize that there are certain actions that are necessary to preserve the family (such as paying bills), or the life of the drinker and others (such as not letting a person drive when intoxicated). Problem-solving, role-playing new responses during the treatment session, and giving specific homework assignments that involve practicing new behaviors are all excellent approaches to implementing these new behaviors.

Family Feedback to the Drinker

A second active intervention is providing direct feedback to the drinker. Families may communicate in unproductive ways about drinking, for example, with nagging, ridicule, and sarcasm. Your goal is to encourage them to use straightforward, constructive communication techniques when giving their feedback. Remember that feedback should be: Provided when the drinker is sober; Factual and objective, rather than evaluative or emotional; Delivered in a caring and compassionate tone, communicating that the family member is discussing drinking out of caring rather than from more negative motives; Associated with specific requests to change.

You can guide family members to develop specific feedback and role-play how to discuss their concerns with the drinking family member.

Family Requests for Change

Family members also can be guided to make specific, positive requests for change from the drinker. Requests may be directed toward changes in the drinking itself, toward behavior when drinking, or toward seeking assistance. You can guide family members in articulating the changes they want and help them practice how to make such requests.

You should prepare the family by explaining that the drinker does not always respond to such discussions or requests with immediate acceptance. You should also help the family understand that requests for change are part of the larger set of behavior changes they have gone through.

Family Support for Change Efforts

Families also need to learn to support the drinker's efforts toward change. They may resist providing support and encouragement, feeling that the drinker is simply doing what he or she "should have done all along." Despite such feelings, support for efforts to change is likely to increase them, while ignoring such efforts or responding negatively likely will decrease attempts at change.

Family members can support change through verbal encouragement, nonverbal gestures, or taking on family responsibilities to free up the drinker's time for treatment or self-help meetings. You can work closely with the family to identify supportive actions that are comfortable and acceptable to them.

Family Member Self-Care

Spouses with an actively drinking partner experience significant levels of anxiety, depression, and psycho-physiological complaints. Children may have behavior problems, anxiety or depression, or eventually develop alcohol or drug problems themselves. Thus, in addition to interventions to attempt to influence the drinker, you should help family members learn how to take care of their own needs.

Twelve-step organizations are one source of support that is specific for families of drinkers. Al-Anon is a self-help organization for adults affected by another's drinking; Alateen provides similar support for adolescents. Al-Anon and Alateen are widely available without cost to participants. The limited amount of research available on Al-Anon has demonstrated its effectiveness in helping to decrease distress among families affected by drinking. Specifically, Al-Anon is most effective as a source of support for the affected family member, and is not designed as a resource for motivating the drinking family member to change. Therefore, you should use this resource primarily as a source of support for affected family members.

Change Through Family-involved Treatment

Two major approaches to family-based treatment for alcohol problems have been developed and tested in controlled research - alcohol-focused behavioral couple's therapy (ABCT), and family systems approaches. ABCT is a structured therapy based on cognitive-behavioral principles of behavior change. Major components of ABCT include:

Cognitive-behavioral strategies that will help the drinker stop drinking and acquire coping skills to respond to both drinking-specific and general life problems; Strategies that teach family members to support the drinker's change efforts, reduce protection for drinking-related consequences, develop better skills to cope with negative affect, and communicate around alcohol-related topics; Strategies to improve the couple's relationship by increasing positive exchanges and improving communication and problem solving skills; Behavioral Contracts between intimate partners to support the use of medication.

Research suggests that ABCT results in greater marital happiness after treatment, fewer incidents of marital separation, and fewer incidents of domestic violence. Many also report that ABCT leads to greater improvements in drinking behavior than comparison treatments, although study results are mixed.

One empirical study has tested the effectiveness of family systems therapy to treat alcohol problems in adults. Family systems therapy views drinking as one aspect of the marital/family relationship and focuses on altering couple interactions that might be sustaining the drinking, as well as each partner's views of the meaning of the drinking.

You may not require abstinence from drinking, but rather may prefer to help couples select and pursue a drinking goal of their own choosing. Both strategic and structural-family therapy techniques can be used to manage clients' ambivalence about change. Preliminary results suggest that such approaches are more effective than cognitive-behavioral approaches in retaining resistant and angry clients in therapy.

Change Through Referral

A second long-term strategy is to refer clients to community-based services for help with their drinking problems. Alcohol treatment services are provided at different levels of care - inpatient, residential rehabilitative, intensive outpatient, outpatient, or self-help.

There are two different approaches to selecting the level of care, and each has some support for its effectiveness.

The first approach is stepped care, in which treatment is initiated at the least restrictive level possible for the client. It is usually a brief, outpatient intervention, and the intensity of treatment is increased only if the client does not respond to the initial intervention.

The second approach, patient-treatment matching, is most fully articulated by the American Society of Addiction Medicine (ASAM) through their patient placement criteria (PPC). The PPC specify six dimensions to consider when selecting an initial level of care:(1) Severity of alcohol dependence and likelihood of withdrawal syndrome; (2) Medical conditions and complications; (3) Emotional/behavioral/cognitive conditions or complications; (4) Motivation to change; (5) Relapse/continued use potential; (6) The nature of the recovery environment.

Although the PPC are quite specific in defining levels of care based on combinations of impairments in these six areas, the general principle underlying the criteria is to select more intensive, supervised treatment for more extensive problems. To effect a referral to the alcohol treatment system, you can obtain information about local treatment resources through your state alcohol and drug agency. Many states provide online treatment directories and/or have toll-free hotlines that provide information about treatment services.

If you anticipate making regular referrals for alcohol treatment, you would do well to visit some of the treatment centers to become familiar with their programs, staff, and facilities. If you expect to effect referrals to individual practitioners, it is appropriate to verify the practitioner's credentials.

Several professions provide specific certifications indicating competence or expertise in substance abuse treatment and/or provide longer term approaches:

Longer-Term Approaches

Mental health providers, including Marriage and Family Therapists (MFT's or MFCC's), may receive national certification from the American Academy of Health Care Providers in the Addictive Disorders.

Counselors may be certified at the state or national level as certified alcohol and drug (or substance abuse) counselors.

Physicians may be certified through the American Society of Addiction Medicine.

Psychiatrists have their own separate certification through the Academy of Addiction Psychiatry.

Psychologists can obtain a Certificate of Proficiency in the Treatment of Substance Use Disorders through the College of Professional Psychology of the American Psychological Association.

Keep in mind that the absence of these certifications does not mean that the practitioner is not skilled in alcohol treatment, but certification does assure that there is a certain level of knowledge and experience.

In addition to knowledge about levels of care and credentials, you also should be aware of research knowledge about effective treatment approaches. Three treatment models have been studied extensively, and each has fairly consistent support for its effectiveness:

Cognitive-Behavioral Therapy (CBT) has been delivered in residential, intensive outpatient, and outpatient settings. CBT focuses on identifying high-risk situations for drinking, developing alternative coping strategies, and preventing relapse. CBT is particularly effective for clients who have less severe alcohol dependence.

Motivational Enhancement Therapy (MET) is a brief, two- to four-session treatment that combines assessment, feedback, and principles of motivational interviewing (described in an earlier section of the Guide). MET is particularly effective for those clients who are angry and resistant at the onset of treatment.

Twelve-Step Facilitation (TSF) treatments are active counseling approaches that draw upon the principles of Alcoholics Anonymous (AA). They help clients develop an affiliation with AA, and work with them through the initial steps. TSF has been provided in residential, intensive outpatient, and outpatient settings, and appears to be particularly effective with clients who have more severe drinking problems, few psychiatric complications, or social networks that encourage them to drink. Treatment programs that draw upon the principles of AA are the most widely available.

Other treatment models and programs also are available, but they lack sufficient research support:

Fairly extensive research literature supports the effectiveness of family systems approaches with adolescents, but limited research has addressed the use of family systems interventions for adults with alcohol use disorders.

Treatment programs exist that are designed specifically for certain populations - women, gay and lesbian clients, people of color, adolescents, and older adults. Although there is compelling evidence of variability in the nature and patterning of drinking and problems in different populations, most population-specific treatment approaches are untested in controlled research studies.

Some programs have incorporated treatment elements to address the unique needs and world views of subgroups of clients, such as spiritual or alternative healing practices, meditation, or nutritional interventions. Empirical bases for these approaches are lacking because they have not been tested in controlled research.

Self Help Groups

Clinicians also should be aware of and familiar with self-help groups.

Alcoholics Anonymous (AA) provides a program of recovery based on twelve steps to recovery that stress acceptance of drinking as a problem, willingness to seek help, and personal and interpersonal change designed to enhance a spiritual approach to life. AA is widely available, free of charge, and requires a desire to stop drinking as the only "membership" requirement. Research studies have found a significant though modest correlation between attending more AA meetings and being abstinent, and an even stronger relationship between involvement with AA (e.g., working the steps, reading AA literature, having a sponsor, as well as going to meetings) and abstinence.

Other self-help groups are less widely available or researched, but provide alternative sources of self-help for clients who would like a self-help format but are unwilling to attend AA. Groups include Women for Sobriety, SMART Recovery, Secular Organizations for Recovery/LifeRing, Moderation Management, and culturally specific .self-help groups, such as Red Road for the American Indian population. Limited research is available about the effectiveness of any of these organizations.

Summary

Alcohol problems are common, particularly among individuals and families seeking mental health services. Families may present other problems as their primary concerns, but drinking is often the primary cause of or corollary to their presenting problems.

Drinking problems may range in severity, from differences in values and preferences about drinking that create family conflicts, to severe alcohol dependence. As a result, marriage and family therapists should screen all clients for possible drinking problems and complete additional assessments where appropriate. When determining whether to intervene and how to intervene, it is important to first consider the overall goals of family therapy and any safety concerns that may be involved. Brief interventions, either directly with the drinker or with concerned family members, can have a positive impact on alcohol problems.

Study Questions

44. According to the BAL estimation chart, a 180 pound adult male with become intoxicated (.08) during his ___ drink.
a. Second
b. Third
c. Fourth
d. Fifth

45. Ultimately, the responsibility for change in drinking rests with:
a. The family
b. The therapist
c. The drinking client
d. None of the above

46. The first step in assessment without the abuser present is:
a. Assessing for safety.
b. Discussing consequences of abusing.
c. Assessing family roles in maintenance of substance abuse behaviors.
d. None of the above.

47. A referral resource/s mentioned in the article:
a. http://findtreatment.samhsa.gov/

b. State alcohol and drug agency
c. 800-622-HELP
d. All of the above

48. The most preferred treatment choice for most clients who have social networks that encourage drinking or abusing drugs:
a. CBT
b. REBT
c. 12 Step
d. Motivational Enhancement Therapy (MET)
e. Go out for a drink.

49. AA is the most widely available 12 step self-help group and is free of charge.
        True   False

50. Unfortunately, brief interventions on alcohol in family therapy rarely help.
        True   False

51. _____ may be useful in helping identify potential alcohol problems in the family.
a. BAL test results
b. Information from collateral reports from Family members
c. The patient's legal record
d. Whether the client has ever attended AA
e. Work record

52. What is co-morbidity?

Answers to Study Questions:
44-c; 45-c; 46-a; 47-d; 48-c; 49-true; 50-false; 51-b; 52- Varies

UNIT 10

How Much is "too much"?

How Much is "Too Much"?

Simply put, drinking becomes too much when it causes or elevates the risk for alcohol related problems or complicates the management of other health problems. Men who drink 5 or more standard drinks in a day (or 15 or more per week) and women who drink 4 or more, in a day (or, 8 or more, per week) are at increased risk for alcohol related problems, according to epidemiologic research.

Individual responses to alcohol vary, however. Drinking at lower levels may be problematic depending on many factors, such as age, coexisting conditions, and medication use. Because it is not known whether any amount of alcohol is safe during pregnancy, the Surgeon General urges abstinence for women who are or may become pregnant.

Why screen for heavy drinking?

At risk drinking and alcohol problems are common. About three in ten U.S. adults drink at levels that elevate their risk for physical, mental health, and social problems. Of these heavy drinkers, about one in four currently has alcohol abuse or dependence. All heavy drinkers have a greater risk of hypertension, gastrointestinal bleeding, sleep disorders, major depression, hemorrhagic stroke, cirrhosis of the liv er, and several cancers.

Heavy drinking often goes undetected. In a recent study of primary care practices, for example, patients with alcohol dependence received the recommended quality of care, including assessment and referral to treatment, only about 10 percent of the time.

As a counselor, you are in a prime position to make a difference. Clinical trials have demonstrated that brief interventions can promote significant, lasting reductions in drinking levels in at risk drinkers who are not alcohol dependent.

Some drinkers who are dependent will accept referral to addiction treatment programs. Even for patients who do not accept a referral, repeated alcohol focused visits with a health provider can lead to significant improvement. If you are not already doing so, you should incorporate alcohol screening, brief intervention, and treatment referral into your practice.

Alcohol Abuse Screening

See the Appendix for the **DrinC** as a basis for the interview. If you find clients who fail to fulfill major role obligations at work, school, or home because of recurrent drinking or who have periods when their drinking—or being sick from drinking—often interfered with taking care of your home or family? Caused job troubles? School problems? Then you have an alcoholic.

Some other areas to check are, and suggested questions:

Recurrent drinking in hazardous situations -
Have you more than once driven a car or other vehicle while you were drinking? Or after having had too much to drink? Have you gotten into situations while drinking or after drinking that increased your chances of getting hurt—like swimming, using machinery, or walking in a dangerous area or around heavy traffic?

Recurrent legal problems related to alcohol -
Have you gotten arrested, been held at a police station, or had any other legal problems because of your drinking? And continued use despite recurrent interpersonal or social problems? Have you continued to drink even though you knew it was causing you trouble with your family or friends? Have you gotten into physical fights while drinking or right after drinking?

Dependence Screening
All the following questions are prefaced by "In the past 12 months..."

Tolerance: Have you found that you have to drink much more than you once did to get the effect you want? Or that your usual number of drinks has much less effect on you than it once did?

Withdrawal syndrome or drinking to relieve withdrawal: When the effects of alcohol are wearing off, have you had trouble sleeping? Found yourself shaking? Nervous? Nauseous? Restless? Sweating or with your heart beating fast? Have you sensed things that aren't really there? Had seizures? Have you taken a drink or used any drug or medicine (other than over the counter pain relievers) to keep from having bad aftereffects of drinking? Or to get over them?

Impaired control: Have you more than once wanted to stop or cut do wn on your drinking? Or tried more than once to stop or cut down but found you couldn't?

Drinking more or longer than intended: Have you had times when you ended up drinking more than you meant to? Or kept on drinking for longer than you intended?

Neglect of activities: In order to drink, have you given up or cut down on activities that were important or interesting to you or gave you pleasure?

Time spent related to drinking or recovering: Have you had a period when you spent a lot of time drinking? Or being sick or getting over the bad aftereffects of drinking?

Continued use despite recurrent psychological or physical problems: Have you continued to drink even though you knew it was making you feel depressed or anxious? Or causing a health problem or making one worse? Or after having had a blackout?

Approach to Brief Intervention

Keep in mind that changing health related behaviors is often a difficult process, with progress interrupted by relapse to less healthy behaviors. Providing reinforcement, support, and thoughtful reflection during an office visit can often make the difference between long term success and failure.

Things to remember when using the General Approach to brief intervention:
- Use a health education approach.
- Be matter of fact and non-confrontational.
- Provide patient education materials.
- Offer choices on how to make changes.
- Emphasize your patient's responsibility for changing drinking behavior.
- Convey confidence in your patient's ability to change drinking behavior

---

Alcohol and Medication Interactions

Alcohol can interact negatively with medications either by interfering with the metabolism of the medication (generally in the liver) or by enhancing the effects of the medication (particularly in the central nervous system). Many classes of prescription medicines can interact with alcohol, including antibiotics, antidepressants, antihistamines, barbiturates, benzodiazepines, histamine H2 receptor agonists, muscle relaxants, non-opioid pain medications and anti-inflammatory agents, opioids, and warfarin. In addition, many over the counter medications and herbal preparations can cause negative side effects when taken with alcohol. Make your clients VERY aware of this, and remind them to check with a physician if they are on major meds. And, since YOU are a not an MD, it is not appropriate for you to advise on actual interactions.

Notes:

UNIT 11

Guidelines for Family Violence and Child Abuse Screening

Guidelines for Family Violence and Child Abuse Screening

Therapists must assess the potential for anger and violence and construct therapy so it can be conducted without endangering any family members. Because of the critical nature of this responsibility, included here are guidelines for the screening of families for violence and neglect

These guidelines have been adapted from a more extensive versions. If during the screening interview, it becomes clear that a batterer is endangering a client or other abuse is occurring in the family, the treatment provider should respond to this situation before any other issue, and if necessary, suspend the rest of the screening interview until the safety of the client or family member can be ensured. The provider should refer the client to a domestic violence program and possibly to a shelter and legal services.

Screening for Domestic Violence and Other Abusive Behavior

To determine if someone has endured domestic violence, look for physical injuries, especially patterns of untreated injuries to the face, neck, and throat.

Other indicators may include:
- Inconsistent explanations for injuries and evasive answers when questioned about them
- Complications in pregnancy, including miscarriage, premature birth, and infant illness or birth defects
- Stress-related illnesses and conditions such as headache, backache, chronic pain, gastrointestinal distress, sleep disorders, eating disorders, and fatigue
- Anxiety-related conditions, such as heart palpitations, hyperventilation, and panic attacks
- A sad, flat affect or talk of suicide
- History of relapse or noncompliance with substance abuse treatment plans

Always interview clients about domestic violence in private. Ask about violence using concrete examples and hypothetical situations rather than vague, conceptual questions. Screening questions should convey to survivors that no battering is justified and that substance abuse is not an acceptable excuse for violent behavior.

Referrals should be made when appropriate for psychotherapy and specialized counseling. Staff training in domestic violence is important so that substance abuse treatment counselors can respond effectively to a domestic violence crisis.

Because batterers in treatment frequently harass their partners, telephone and visitation privileges of batterers and survivors in residential substance abuse treatment programs should be carefully monitored.

A good initial question to investigate the possibility that a client is abusing family members is, "Do you think violence against a partner is justified in some situations?" A third-person example may be used, followed by specific, concrete questions that define the extent of the violence:

- What happens when you lose your temper?
- When you hit [name of family member], was it a slap or a punch?
- Do you take car keys away? Damage property?
- Threaten to injure or kill [name of family member]?

Once it has been confirmed that a client has been abusive, whether physically, sexually, or psychologically, the provider should contact a domestic violence expert, either for referral or consultation. Treatment providers should ensure that the danger the batterer poses is carefully assessed.

Become familiar with batterers' rationalizations and excuses for their behavior:

- Minimizing: "I only pushed her." "She exaggerates."
- Claiming good intentions: "When she gets hysterical, I have to slap her or hold her, to calm her down."
- Blaming intoxication: "I'm not myself when I drink."
- Pleading loss of control: "I can only take so much." "I was so angry, I didn't know what I was doing."
- Faulting the partner: "She drove me to it." "She really knows how to get to me."
- Shifting blame to someone or something else: "I was raised that way." "My probation officer is putting a lot of pressure on me." "I've been out of work."

Screening for Child Abuse

Federal and State laws require health care providers, and in some cases "any person" to report suspected child abuse or neglect. Consequently, substance abuse treatment providers must notify a child protective services agency if they suspect child abuse or neglect. Providers that fail to carry out this mandate are subject to loss of license, fines, or imprisonment, as well as civil liability. In order to avoid any client feeling that they have been betrayed, notification regarding Federal and State reporting requirements should be clearly stated during the admission process, and should be prominently written or stated for those parts of any treatment program that involve participation of the client's family, friends, or others.

When discussing the limits of confidentiality, treatment programs should be sure that clients understand that those requirements do not affect the absolute reporting requirement of suspected child abuse or neglect. Clients should understand that their permission is not needed in any way, as child abuse or neglect reporting laws must be adhered to regardless of the concerns of the client or others.

During initial screening, the interviewer should attempt to determine whether a client's children have been physically or emotionally harmed and whether their behavior has changed. Have they become mute? Do they scream, cry, or act out?

The substance abuse treatment provider should not assess children for abuse or incest. Only personnel with special expertise should perform this delicate function (e.g., a psychologist, psychiatrist, social worker, or other care provider authorized by State child protective services). The treatment provider should, however, note any indications of child abuse occurring in a client's household and pass these suspicions on to the appropriate agency.

Indications of child abuse that can crop up in a client interview include:
- A protective services agency has been involved with anyone who lives in the home
- The children's behaviors are indicative of abuse (e.g., bedwetting, sexual acting out)
- Extraordinary closeness is noted between a child and another adult in the household
- The client reports blackouts (batterers often claim to black out during a violent episode)

If a treatment provider suspects that a client's child has been abused, the provider must immediately refer the child to a health care provider. If the parent will not take the child to a doctor (who is required by law to report suspected abuse), the provider must contact home health services or child protective services.

If the treatment provider reports suspected or definite child abuse or neglect, the provider must assess the impact on any client also being battered and develop a safety plan if one is deemed necessary. Providers should be aware that if a child has been or is being abused by the mother's partner, it is likely that the mother is also being abused.

Notes:

Affect: Feeling or emotion, especially as manifested by facial expression or body language.

Boundary: An invisible though often effective barrier within a relationship that governs the level of contact. Boundaries can appropriately shape and regulate relationships. Two dysfunctional types of boundaries are those that are (1) so rigid, inhibiting meaningful interaction so that the people in the relationship are said to be "disengaged" from each other, or (2) so loose that individuals lose a sense of independence so that the "enmeshed" relationship stifles individuality and initiative.

Complementarity: A pattern of human interactions in which partners in an intimate relationship establish roles and take on behavioral patterns that fulfill the unconscious needs and demands of the other.

Disengagement: The state of being unreachably aloof or distant from others.

Enmeshment: The state of being in which two people are so close emotionally that one perceives the other as "smothering" him or her with affection, concern, attention, etc. Enmeshment also can occur without a conscious sense of it.

Family Structure: Repeated, predictable patterns of interaction between family members that influence individual behavior to a considerable extent.

Family Therapy: An approach to therapy based on the idea that a family is—and behaves as—a system. Interventions are based on the presumption that when one part of the system changes, other parts will change in response. Family therapists therefore look for unhealthy structures and faulty patterns of communication.

Homeostasis: A natural process in which multigenerational competing forces seek to maintain a state of equilibrium (i.e., balance).

Integrated Models: A constellation of interventions that takes into account (1) each family member's issues as they relate to the substance abuse and (2) the effect of each member's issues on the family system.

Phases of Family Change: A model of family change that includes three elements occurring in a series: attainment of sobriety, adjustment to sobriety, and long-term maintenance of sobriety.

Triangulation: This occurs when two family members dealing with a problem come to a place where they need to discuss a sensitive issue. Instead of facing the issue, they divert their energy to a third member who acts as a go-between, scapegoat, object of concern, or ally. By involving this other person, they reduce their emotional tension, but prevent their conflict from being resolved and miss opportunities to increase the intimacy in their relationship.

Notes:

APPENDIX

Genograms

One technique used by family therapists to help them understand family relations is the genogram, a pictorial chart of the people involved in a three-generational relationship system, marking marriages, divorces, births, geographical location, deaths, and illness.

Though the preparation of a genogram is not standardized, most of them begin with the legal and biological relationships of family members. Different genogram styles search out different information and use different symbols to depict relationships. For instance, a **family map** is a variation that arranges family members in relation to a specific problem (such as substance abuse). Genograms can help family members see themselves and their relationships in a new way, and can be a useful tool for substance abuse treatment providers who want to understand how family relationships affect clients and their substance abuse.

Basically, a GENOGRAM is a pictorial chart of the people involved in a three-generational relationship system, marking marriages, divorces, births, geographical location, deaths, and illness. Significant physical, social, and psychological dysfunction may be added. A Genogram assists the therapist in understanding the family and is used to examine a family's relationships.

The 25-item Alcohol Dependence Scale (ADS)

INSTRUCTIONS:

Carefully read each question and the possible answers provided. Answer each question by circling the ONE choice that is most true for you. The word "drinking" in a question refers to "drinking of alcoholic beverages."

Take as much time as you need. Work carefully, and try to finish as soon as possible. Please answer ALL questions.

THESE QUESTIONS REFER TO THE PAST 12 MONTHS.

1. How much did you drink the last time you drank?
   a. Enough to get high or less
   b. Enough to get drunk
   c. Enough to pass out

2. Do you often have hangovers on Sunday or Monday mornings?
   a. No   b. Yes

3. Have you had the "shakes" when sobering up(hands tremble, shake inside)?
   a. No   b. Sometimes   c. Often

4. Do you get physically sick (e.g., vomit, stomach cramps) as a result of drinking?
   a. No
   b. Sometimes
   c. Almost every time I drink

5. Have you had the "DTs" (delirium tremens) - that is, seen, felt or heard things not really there; ever felt very anxious, restless, and over excited?
   a. No   b. Yes

6. When you drink, do you stumble about, stagger, and weave?
   a. No
   b. Sometimes
   c. Often

7. As a result of drinking, have you felt overly hot and sweaty (feverish)?
   a. No
   b. Once
   c. Several times

8. As a result of drinking, have you seen things that were not really there?
    a. No
    b. Once
    c. Several times

9. Do you panic because you fear you may not have a drink when you need it?
    a. No   b. Yes

10. Have you had blackouts ("loss of memory" without passing out) as a result of drinking?
    a. No, never
    b. Sometimes
    c. Often
    d. Almost every time I drink

11. Do you carry a bottle with you or keep one close at hand?
    a. No
    b. Some of the time
    c. Most of the time

12. After a period of abstinence (not drinking), do you end up drinking heavily again?
    a. No
    b. Sometimes
    c. Almost every time I drink

13. In the past 12 months, have you passed out as a result of drinking?
    a. No
    b. Once
    c. More than once

14. Have you had a convulsion (fit) following a period of drinking?
    a. No
    b. Yes
    c. Several times

15. Do you drink throughout the day?
    a. No   b. Yes

16. After drinking heavily, has your thinking been fuzzy or unclear?
    a. No

b. Yes, but only for a few hours
c. Yes, for one or two days
d. Yes, for many days

17. As a result of drinking, have you felt your heart beating rapidly?
    a. No
    b. Yes
    c. Several times

18. Do you almost constantly think about drinking and alcohol?
    a. No   b. Yes

19. As a result of drinking, have you heard "things"that were not really there?
    a. No
    b. Yes
    c. Several times

20. Have you had weird and frightening sensations when drinking?
    a. No
    b. Once or twice
    c. Often

21. As a result of drinking have you "felt things" crawling on you that were not really there (e.g., bugs, spiders)?
    a. No
    b. Yes
    c. Several times

22. With respect to blackouts (loss; of memory):
    a. Have never had a blackout
    b. Have had blackouts that last less than an hour
    c. Have had blackouts that last for several hours
    d. Have had blackouts that last a day or more

23. Have you tried to cut down on your drinking failed?
    a. No
    b. Once
    c. Several times

24. Do you gulp drinks (drink quickly?)

a. No   b. Yes

25. After taking one or two drinks, can you usually stop?
    a. Yes   b. No

   The ADS can be used in wide variety of settings for screening and assessment of alcohol dependence. The ADS can be used for screening and case finding in a variety of settings including health care, corrections, general population surveys, workplace, and education. A score of 9 or more is highly predictive of DSM diagnosis of alcohol dependence.

Scoring: No/Yes items are scored 0/1; three-choice items are scored 0, 1, 2; and four-choice items are
scored 0, 1, 2, 3. In each case, the higher the value the greater the dependence. Total scores can range from 0 to 47.

Severity of Alcohol Dependence Questionnaire (Sadq-c)

Please recall a typical period of heavy drinking in the last 6 months. When was this?
Month :   Year :

Please answer all the following questions about your drinking by circling your most appropriate response.

During that period of heavy drinking:

1. The day after drinking alcohol, I woke up feeling sweaty.
ALMOST/ NEVER/ SOMETIMES/ OFTEN/ NEARLY ALWAYS

2. The day after drinking alcohol, my hands shook first thing in the morning.
ALMOST/ NEVER/ SOMETIMES/ OFTEN/ NEARLY ALWAYS

3. The day after drinking alcohol, my whole body shook violently first thing in the morning if I didn't have a drink.
ALMOST/ NEVER/ SOMETIMES/ OFTEN/ NEARLY ALWAYS

4. The day after drinking alcohol, I woke up absolutely drenched in sweat.
ALMOST/ NEVER/ SOMETIMES/ OFTEN/ NEARLY ALWAYS

5. The day after drinking alcohol, I dread waking up in the morning.
ALMOST/ NEVER/ SOMETIMES/ OFTEN/ NEARLY ALWAYS

6. The day after drinking alcohol, I was frightened of meeting people first thing in the morning.
ALMOST/ NEVER/ SOMETIMES/ OFTEN/ NEARLY ALWAYS

7. The day after drinking alcohol, I felt at the edge of despair when I awoke.
ALMOST/ NEVER/ SOMETIMES/ OFTEN/ NEARLY ALWAYS

8. The day after drinking alcohol, I felt very frightened when I awoke.
ALMOST/ NEVER/ SOMETIMES/ OFTEN/ NEARLY ALWAYS

9. The day after drinking alcohol, I liked to have an alcoholic drink in the morning.
ALMOST/ NEVER/ SOMETIMES/ OFTEN/ NEARLY ALWAYS

10. The day after drinking alcohol, I always gulped my first few alcoholic drinks down as quickly as possible.
ALMOST/ NEVER/ SOMETIMES/ OFTEN/ NEARLY ALWAYS

11. The day after drinking alcohol, I drank alcohol to get rid of the shakes.
ALMOST/ NEVER/ SOMETIMES/ OFTEN/ NEARLY ALWAYS

12. The day after drinking alcohol, I had a very strong craving for a drink when I awoke.
ALMOST/ NEVER/ SOMETIMES/ OFTEN/ NEARLY ALWAYS

13. I drank more than a quarter of a bottle of spirits in a day (OR 1 bottle of wine OR 7 beers).
ALMOST/ NEVER/ SOMETIMES/ OFTEN/ NEARLY ALWAYS

14. I drank more than half a bottle of spirits per day (Or 2 bottles of wine Or 15 beers).
ALMOST/ NEVER/ SOMETIMES/ OFTEN/ NEARLY ALWAYS

15. I drank more than one bottle of spirits per day (Or 4 bottles of wine Or 30 beers).
ALMOST/ NEVER/ SOMETIMES/ OFTEN/ NEARLY ALWAYS

16. I drank more than two bottles of spirits per day (Or 8 bottles of wine Or 60 beers).
ALMOST/ NEVER/ SOMETIMES/ OFTEN/ NEARLY ALWAYS

For the rest of the Questions, imagine the following situation :
You have been completely off drink for a few weeks. You then drink very heavily for two days —
How would you feel the morning after those two days of drinking?

17. I would start to sweat.
NOT AT ALL/ SLIGHTLY/ MODERATELY/ QUITE A LOT

18. My hands would shake.
NOT AT ALL/ SLIGHTLY/ MODERATELY/ QUITE A LOT

19. My body would shake.
NOT AT ALL/ SLIGHTLY/ MODERATELY/ QUITE A LOT

20. I would be craving for a drink.
NOT AT ALL/ SLIGHTLY/ MODERATELY/ QUITE A LOT

The Severity of Alcohol Dependence Questionnaire was developed by the Addiction Research Unit at the Maudsley Hospital. It is a measure of the severity of dependence.

Scoring: 0 / 1 / 2 / 3
A score of 31 or higher indicates severe alcohol dependence.
A score of 16-30 indicates moderate dependence.
A score of below 16 usually indicates only a mild physical dependency.
A detoxification regime is usually indicated for someone who scores 16 or over.

Drinker Inventory of Consequences(DrInC)

INSTRUCTIONS: Here are a number of events that drinkers sometimes experience. Read each one carefully, and circle the number that indicates whether, to the best of your knowledge, this has happened to the person about whom you are concerned.

Part ONE

Since the last interview or time you talked with the counselor, about how often has this happened to the person?

Circle one answer:(0) Never (1) Once or a few times (2) Once or twice a week (3) Daily or almost daily

1. They had a hangover or felt bad after drinking.
    0   1   2   3
2. They missed days of work or school because of drinking.
    0   1   2   3
3. Their family or friends have worried or complained about their drinking.
    0   1   2   3
4. The quality of their work has suffered because of drinking.
    0   1   2   3
5. Their ability to be a good parent has been harmed by drinking.
    0   1   2   3
6. Thye have driven a motor vehicle after having three or more drinks.
    0   1   2   3
7. They have been sick and vomited after drinking.
    0   1   2   3
8. Because of their drinking, they have not eaten properly.
    0   1   2   3
9. They have failed to do what is expected of them because of drinking.
    0   1   2   3
10. While drinking, they have said or done embarrassing things.
    0   1   2   3
11. When drinking, their personality has changed for the worse.
    0   1   2   3
12. They have taken foolish risks when drinking.
    0   1   2   3

115

Part TWO
SINCE THE LAST INTERVIEW, about how often has this happened to them?
Circle one answer: (0) Never; (1) Once or a few times;
(2) Once or twice a week; (3) Daily or almost daily

13. They have gotten into trouble because of drinking.
    0   1   2   3
14. When drinking, they have said harsh or cruel things to someone.
    0   1   2   3

15. When drinking, they have done impulsive things that were regretted later.
    0   1   2   3
16. They have gotten into a physical fight while drinking.
    0   1   2   3

Part THREE
Now answer these questions about things that may have happened to them SINCE THE LAST INTERVIEW.
Circle one answer: (0)Not at all; (1) A little;
(2) Somewhat; (3) Very much

17. Their physical health has been harmed by drinking.
    0   1   2   3
18. They have had money problems because of drinking.
    0   1   2   3
19. Their marriage or love relationship has been harmed by drinking.
    0   1   2   3
20. Their physical appearance has been harmed by drinking.
    0   1   2   3
21. Their family has been hurt by drinking.
    0   1   2   3
22. A friendship or close relationship of theirs has been damaged by drinking.
    0   1   2   3
23. They are overweight because of their drinking.
    0   1   2   3
24. They have lost interest in activities and hobbies because of drinking.

     0   1   2   3

25. Drinking has damaged their social life, popularity, or reputation.
     0   1   2   3

26. They have spent too much or lost a lot of money because of drinking.
     0   1   2   3

Part FOUR

Has this happened to him SINCE THE LAST INTERVIEW?
Circle one answer:
(0) No; (1) Almost; (2) Yes, Once; (3) Yes, more than once

27. They have been arrested for driving under the influence of alcohol.
     0   1   2   3
28. Had trouble with the law (other than driving while intoxicated) because of drinking.
     0   1   2   3
29. Lost a marriage or a close love relationship because of drinking.
     0   1   2   3
30. Been suspended/fired from or left a job or school because of drinking.
     0   1   2   3
31. Lost a friend because of drinking.
     0   1   2   3
32. Had an accident while drinking or intoxicated.
     0   1   2   3
33. While drinking or intoxicated has been physically hurt, injured, or burned.
     0   1   2   3
34. While drinking or intoxicated has injured someone else.
     0   1   2   3
35. Has broken things or damaged property while drinking or intoxicated.
     0   1   2   3

RESOURCES

Adult Children of Alcoholics (ACA) World Services Organization, Inc. P.O. Box 3216 Torrance, CA 90510 Phone: (310) 534-1815 Web site: www.adultchildren.org

Adult Children of Alcoholics is a 12-Step, 12 Tradition program of men and women who grew up in alcoholic or otherwise dysfunctional homes.

Adult Children Anonymous, ACA General Service Network P.O. Box 25166 Minneapolis, MN 55458
Web site: www.12stepforums.net/acoa.html

Adult Children Anonymous is a 12-Step program modeled after Alcoholics Anonymous. It is a spiritual program designed to help adults raised in families where either substance addiction, mental illness, or generalized dysfunction was present.

Al- Anon and Alateen/ Al-Anon Family Group Headquarters, Inc. 1600 Corporate Landing Parkway Virginia Beach, VA 23454 Phone: (757) 563-1600 Fax: (757) 563-1655 Web site: www.al-anon.org

Al-Anon is a group of relatives and friends of alcoholics who share their experience, strength, and hope to solve their common problems. The purpose of Al-Anon is to help families of alcoholics by practicing the 12 steps, by welcoming and giving comfort, and by providing understanding and encouragement.

Alateen, which can be contacted through Al-Anon, is a group made up of young Al-Anon members, usually teenagers, whose lives have been affected by someone else's drinking.

American Association for Marriage and Family Therapy (AAMFT) 112 South Alfred Street Alexandria, VA 22314 Phone: (703) 838-9808 Fax: (703) 838-9805 Web site: www.aamft.org

The American Association for Marriage and Family Therapy represents the professional interests of more than 23,000 marriage and family therapists throughout the United States, Canada, and abroad.

Co-Anon Family Groups/ Co-Anon Family Groups World Services P.O. Box 12722 Tucson, AZ 85732 Phone: (800) 898-9985; (520) 513-5028 Web site: www.co-anon.org

Co-Anon Family Groups are a fellowship of men and women who are husbands, wives, parents, relatives, or close friends of someone who is chemically dependent.

Co-Dependents Anonymous, Inc. (CoDA) P.O. Box 33577 Phoenix, AZ 85067 Web site: www.codependents.org

Co-Dependents Anonymous, Inc. is a fellowship of men and women whose common purpose is to develop healthy relationships. CoDA relies on the 12 Steps and 12 Traditions for knowledge and wisdom.

Families Anonymous P.O. Box 3475 Culver City, CA 90231 Infoline: (800) 736-

119

9805 Fax: (310) 815-9682
Web site: familiesanonymous.org. Families Anonymous is a nonprofit organization that provides emotional support for relatives and friends of individuals with substance or behavioral problems using the 12 steps.

The National Association for Children of Alcoholics (NACoA), 11426 Rockville Pike, Suite 100 Rockville, MD 20852, Web site: nacoa.org. NACoA is a national nonprofit membership organization working on behalf of children whose parents have substance use disorders. NACoA's mission is to advocate for all children and families affected by alcoholism and other drug dependencies.

National Center on Substance Abuse and Child Welfare (NCSACW). Web site: ncsacw.samhsa.gov E-mail questions to ncsacw@samhsa.gov. The National Center on Substance Abuse and Child Welfare is an initiative of DHHS and jointly funded by SAMHSA, CSAT, and the Administration on Children, Youth and Families, Children's Bureau's Office on Child Abuse and Neglect.

One of NCSACW's primary goals is to develop materials and resources that serve to advance knowledge and practice in the linkages among substance abuse, child welfare, and family court systems. A wealth of products and services— including curricula, tutorials, and training materials, publications, technical assistance, and presentations—can be accessed via its Web site.

U.S. Department of Health and Human Services Families & Children Web Site Web site: dhhs.gov/children/index.shtml. This Web site provides information and resources for and about families and children under several categories, including adoption, babies, children, family issues (child support, child care, domestic violence, child abuse), low-income families, DHHS agencies, immunizations/vaccinations, kids' Web sites, pregnancy, safety and wellness, teenagers, teen Web sites, and other resources.

Special Thanks to:

**Alexey, Andi, Aunt Lil,
Camille, Fred, Georgia,
Harriet, Janette, Kazuki, Monti,
Matt, Muff, Rod, Ross, Shirley,
Tom, and Valentin
2016**

******

Remembering

Made in the USA
Lexington, KY
22 September 2016